CW00697038

Stock Market Blueprint for the Diligent Investor

Proven strategies for consistently making money on the stock
market without quitting your day job

By

Deji Oduli

Stock Market Blueprint for the Diligent Investor

Published in the United Kingdom by Chaste Investments

ISBN 978-0-9564247-0-9

Warning and Disclaimer

Table of Contents

Dedication and Acknowledgement

I dedicate this book to my wife Bola, for the encouragement and support and for being the first editor of the book; to my daughters Tanitoluwa, Seyifunmi and Seyitan for letting 'daddy' get on with his work; and to my parents for investing so heavily in me.

I'll like to acknowledge the effort of everyone that has contributed to the successful publication of this book. It's not possible to mention everyone, but I'll like to say a big thank you to Dr Albert Odulele for the encouragement and inspiration.

I'll also like to thank God for good health, strength and all the wonderful things He has done in my life.

Foreword

'Stock Market Blueprint, for the Diligent Investor' is a timely book in a global economic climate reeling from one financial storm after the other. Several national economies are still in recession, local and international businesses struggle to stay afloat, reputable banks are being bailed out and individuals have never had to live in an atmosphere of such serious economic peril.

Continuing business as usual is unacceptable. Maintaining the status quo is not an option and fundamentalist fiscal thinking has never been as challenged as it is now. The prevailing global atmosphere is compelling and forces the average employee to seek reasonable, safe investment opportunities. Wisdom dictates that working class people should find multiple income streams and this book presents you with an option to intelligently consider.

Several years ago I invested in the Stock Market and lost a huge sum of money. It was a harrowing experience that taught me never to invest in anything uninformed or unprepared. 'Stock Market Blueprint' is designed to help the 'layman' navigate the treacherous waters of ignorance, greed and haste. It is a brilliant tool for the serious minded, level headed 'would be' stock market investor.

Deji Odusi has removed the mystique and opened the world of stock market opportunities to the ordinary man or woman out there. Every home keeper, fishmonger, student, bus driver, teacher, nurse, etc can be an investor; and an intelligent successful one too. Put in his own words, 'you do not need to be a stock market or economics expert to make money in stocks and shares'.

As a medical doctor and man of the cloth, I read this book with fascination and keen interest. I was both enlightened and empowered at the same time. It allayed the scepticism of the past, simplified the process and explained the science, psychology, discipline and wisdom required for successful stock market investing. I highly recommend the writ and the writer.

Dr Albert Odulele

MB ChB; PhD

Glory House Churches International

Introduction

"There is only one way to make a great deal of money, and that is in a business of your own."

--J. Paul Getty, oil tycoon

This book is a product of over 5 years of research, trials and experience. Like most people I started out trying to find the "Holy Grail" of stock market investing. It took a while before I realised there was no such thing as a "Holy Grail" in the stock market.

As I began to invest, I started to note down what worked for me as an individual. I discovered that because I had a full time job in another profession, I couldn't just follow the advice of people that monitor the stock market all day long, and expect to get the same results that they get. I also needed a system that would not take away my peace and prevent me from sleeping at night. I've taken everything that I learned and I have presented the strategies and principles that work best in this book.

I have written this book to serve as an introduction for people that are new to the stock market and also as a reference for people that are already involved in the stock market. The book has been written in a very easy to understand format.

The principles that are outlined in this book can also serve as a guide to validating a stock broker's or financial adviser's recommendations because at the end of the day the onus of making a financial decision is on the investor, not the stock broker. The small print in every brochure reminds an investor that the value of an investment can rise or fall i.e. there is no guarantee that it will rise. The broker or financial adviser takes no responsibility for losses incurred on an investment. Bearing this in mind, it is good for an investor to have the tools to perform a due diligence on any recommendation before committing to it. This book provides such tools.

This is not a 'get rich quick' book. Investing in the stock market requires diligence and patience. There are no short cuts. This book contains strategies that can be used to build wealth over a period of time. I hope that through this book you'll develop a blueprint that works for you.

Should you be investing in the stock market by yourself?

Please note that investing in the stock market is a business, not a pastime. Before you start using this book you might want to ask yourself whether you should spend time studying charts and making your own decisions about what shares to buy or sell, or whether you should just open up a managed investment account with a broker and leave the decisions to the broker.

Thousands of investors have taken the bold step to actually investing by themselves. Should you be investing (i.e., buying and selling shares) based on your own personal research, or should you just trust your stockbroker or an investment fund to do it for you? There is no right or wrong answer to this question. It all depends on your personality and your long term goals, amongst other things. Personally I'm of the opinion that you should do both. You should put some money towards an investment fund or vehicle, and you should also have a do-it-yourself portfolio or fund.

A question that might come to your mind is "why do I need to have a do-it-yourself portfolio"? As Peter Lynch put it in *One Up on Wall Street*, "*Rule #1, in my book, is: stop listening to professionals. Twenty years in this business convinces me that any normal person using the customary three per cent of the brain can pick stocks just as well, if not better, than the average Wall Street expert. Think like an amateur...If you're a surfer, a truck driver, a high school dropout, or an eccentric retiree, then you've got an edge already.*" Another notable quote by Peter Lynch is "*Everyone has the brainpower to follow the stock market. If you made it through fifth-grade math, you can do it.*"

You can build a winning mutual fund portfolio by yourself, because all of the expertise and information you need is now available to you. Wall Street's (or the Square mile's) historic monopoly over financial information no longer exists - investors today are not dependent on their brokers for tips or information resources. The power has shifted to individual investors.

Individual investors have the potential to vastly outperform both fund managers and the market. Research has shown that only a handful of fund managers outperform the stock market. In fact, most fund managers have not got the flexibility that individual investors have got. Am I saying that fund managers are useless or that they do not know what they are doing? No! Am I saying that individual investors are smarter than fund managers? No! With all due respect, the average fund manager has an above average IQ. They need to have the ability to digest a lot of complicated information, and they manage millions of pounds. In fact, they need to have a certain type of psychology that individual investors do not possess.

However, before you start investing for yourself, you need to make sure that you have the patience to sit still, i.e. ride the trend in the market. You need to be disciplined and have the self control to invest/trade according to your written down plan. You also need to be confident in your ability to invest. Finally, you need to spare time to read and research on shares and strategies for buying shares.

Most people put too much emphasis on brains. Lots of people think, "I'm smart, I can do it", but it's weaknesses in the other areas that will affect your performance. I have seen a lot of doctors and engineers lose thousands of pounds in the stock market. They think they are smart and buying shares is as easy as A-B-C, but soon find out that the stock market is not a respecter of qualifications. I have also seen people that have no formal qualifications make thousands in the stock market. In fact, success in the stock market is accredited more to psychology than intelligence.

However, before you call up a stock broker or go online to open an account, ask yourself these questions; "Do I have the time?", "Is it really worth the time?", "Am I willing to take that risk?"

Why most people don't invest in the stock market

Most people do not invest in the stock market because they think that it is a complex concept which should be left to people that are gifted in mathematics. They think that they need to be experts in topics like Price/Earnings ratio, net book value, EPS, yields etc. These are concepts you need to understand if you are an investor that looks into the fundamentals of a company. If you are a private investor you can use other means to analyse shares. We would be looking at the alternative method in this book. It is called technical analysis. Even though it is called technical analysis, it is not rocket science. It is easy to use but requires a lot of discipline.

The concepts in this book can also be used to validate broker tips and recommendations

Let me reveal a secret to you. The truth is that even if you rely on a stock broker to make recommendations for you, you accept the recommendation at your own risk. Like I mentioned earlier, stock brokers remind you that share prices might go up or down and that you are not guaranteed a positive return on your investment. If that is the case, shouldn't you be able to perform your own analysis before committing money to a stock? This book would provide you with some of the tools that you can use. Let me give you examples of where I had saved myself from bad investments because I was able to analyse stocks.

In May 2008 a broker called me up to recommend that I buy shares in one of the largest UK banks. At the time the shares were selling for around £5. I told him that I had to do my own due diligence and asked him to call me later for my decision. During my free time I went to check the charts for the bank he recommended and noticed that the share price was actually in a downtrend. When he called back I told him that I wouldn't buy the bank and gave him my reasons. He responded by trying to convince me that the shares were cheap and that was the best time. To cut a long story short, I stood my ground and did not buy. By the end of the year shares in that bank were selling at around £1.50.

In a similar scenario, In July 2008, I was watching one of the popular financial channels and they were interviewing a stock analyst. The analyst was recommending that people buy shares in the solar energy sector. He mentioned a couple of the solar companies that he was sure their share prices were going to rise. He gave some fundamental reasons why the prices would go up. Again, to cut a long story short, shares in solar energy companies actually tanked (fell) within three months of his recommendations. One of the stocks he recommended was cost around $60 at the time. By October of the same year those shares cost around $20. However, looking at the charts I knew this would happen.

Reasons why you might want to invest or earn money from the stock market

1. **To save towards a child's education, especially university.** I was reading an article in the papers recently and the article was talking about how parents would have to save towards a child's university education from the day a child is born. At the moment (2009) university fees are capped at £3,225 in the UK, however many vice chancellors are proposing that it is raised to £7,000 per year. Some are even proposing that top universities should be privatised and be able to charge whatever they like. To reduce the burden of student loan debts on their children, parents should save, or better still, invest towards funding their children's university fee.
2. **Investing towards retirement.** We all know that company pensions cannot totally be relied on now. If you want to find out why, go and talk to people that worked for companies that went bust. Some people contributed towards a pension for over 15 years, yet don't know whether they would be getting anything out of it. If you want to secure your future, you can start your own "pension plan", by investing. In the UK, the government allows individuals to do this through a SIPP plan.
3. **As an additional stream of income.** This is a very common reason for investing in the stock market. In fact most self made millionaires had or have additional streams of income. It is very rear to become financially independent from just one source of income

Keep It Simple S.........

The aim of this book is to keep your investment strategy simple. As the acronym goes, KISS. Some people like to make their investment complicated by using too many indicators, but in reality a complex system is almost impossible to use. When systems are too complex people tend to want to cut corners. When systems are complex, people deviate from them. Deviating from a system means you won't get the results you should be getting.

Although there are hundreds of chart patterns and technical indicators that investors can use to generate their buy and sell signals, this book will concentrate on a few chart patterns and four major technical indicators. These indicators if used correctly will produce consistent positive results. In fact, a major investment research institution performed a study of some indicators and concluded that one of the indicators covered in this book, the moving average convergence divergence indicator, proved to be one of the most reliable indicators.

It's a Global Stock Market

Even though this book uses examples from the UK and the US stock markets, the book is targeted at a global audience. The Internet has made the stock market a global marketplace and you do not necessarily need to reside in a country to be able to partake in the country's stock market. For instance you can be residing in the Republic of Ireland and partake in the UK stock market. Likewise you can be residing in the UK and be an active investor in the US stock market. You can also be resident in Africa and still be an active participant in the European stock market.

How to use this book

To gain maximum benefit from this book you might need to go through it more than once. You should try and take notes as you go along. You might not gain full understanding of some technical terms first time round, but as you go through it again a lot of things will become clearer. If you are new to trading or the stock market, please go through the entire book before you start investing. I have included a lot of quotes in the book, don't just read the quotes, try and reflect on them.

For the purpose of this book the terms investing and trading have been used interchangeably.

"I believe that anyone who is intelligent, conscientious, and willing to put in the necessary time can be successful on Wall Street. As long as they realize the market is a business like any other business, they have a good chance to prosper."

- Jesse Livermore

Chapter 1

The New Stock Market

The key to building wealth is to preserve capital and wait patiently for the right opportunity to make extraordinary gains."

- Victor Sperandeo

The Way to Invest in the Stock Market has Changed

The way to invest in the stock market has changed. The practice of buying shares and holding onto them for a long time is no longer the best way to invest. In today's stock market the people that profit the most are those that can accurately identify when to buy and when to sell. Share prices move in cycles and in trends.

As mentioned earlier, in today's stock market, buying and holding a share over a long period of time does not yield the best returns for an investor. Even when you take dividends into consideration it's still more profitable to be a short-term or medium-term investor/trader. Investors that bought shares in 1998 and are still holding onto those shares today are holding onto shares whose value is a lot less than what they paid. To get a clearer picture of what I'm saying take a look at the following charts.

Take a look at figure 1.1 and you will notice that the share price of Barclays in October 2008 is much less than it was in 1999. However, the share price did not fall continuously throughout the period because there were times when it was rising. Between 2003 and 2007, the share price rose from 350p to 750p, an increase of over 100%. Savvy investors try and identify periods when the share prices are rising, buy quality shares during that period. They also study charts or market conditions to know when share prices are about to fall and they sell most of their shares during the downward move and keep their cash in hand and wait for the next upward move. Using the figure 1.1 to illustrate, intelligent investors would have sold most of their Barclays holdings at the beginning of 2007.

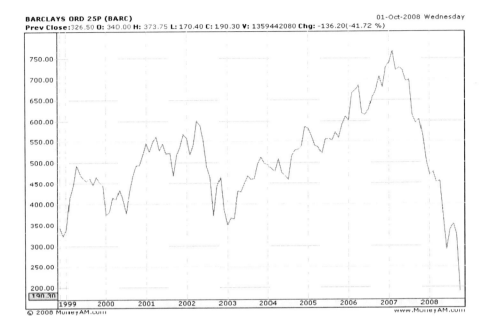

BARCLAYS ORD 25P (BARC)   01-Oct-2008 Wednesday
Prev Close:326.50 O: 340.00 H: 373.75 L: 170.40 C: 190.30 V: 1359442080 Chg: -136.20(-41.72 %)

Figure 1.1

Also take a look at the figure 1.2 and you'll notice that Pfizer's share price in October 2008 was the same value as it was 10 years before. Savvy investors would have bought Pfizer shares during the uptrend and sold during the downtrend.

In today's stock market, share prices move in cycles. Some shares tend to have a good month, a good quarter, or a good year. The same shares that had a good month in January and February might have a bad month in March. To profit in the stock market you have to be able to identify the cycles and patterns of the stock. You can do this by learning how to read and interpret charts. Even though this might look like a very easy process, a lot of people get it wrong and end up losing rather than making money.

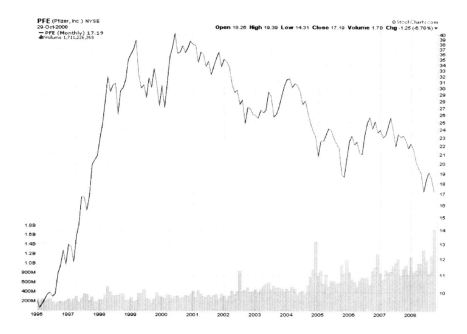

Figure 1.2

Figure 1.3 shows how you can buy shares and sell a few days or weeks later. You could have bought BP shares at 510p in January and sold them about 3 weeks later at around 570p. That is a profit of around 60p per share. If you bought 500 shares, that will be a profit of £300 within 3 weeks. Did you know that you don't need to have the entire deposit of £2,550 (i.e. 510p * 500) to be able to hold 500 shares of BP? You can use something called "leverage". You would pay a small deposit to hold and equivalent of 500 shares of BP (or any other share). You can do this using "leverage". We would talk about this later.

Even though the chart looks simple, there are strategies that you need to know. The strategies covered in this book will show how you can identify trends and movements in share prices.

BP $0.25 (BP.)   20-May-2008 Tuesday
Prev Close:643.00 **O:** 640.50 **H:** 645.00 **L:** 628.00 **C:** 628.00 **V:** 123061826 **Chg:** -15.00(-2.33 %)

Figure 1.3

Thinking outside the Box

In today's stock market, you can also make money when share prices are falling. You have to be creative in your thinking and be able to think outside the box. You make money while share prices are falling by selling shares that you do not own. The process is called "short selling" or "selling short". Take a look at the Northern Rock chart in figure 1.4. It shows the price movements of shares in Northern Rock. While a lot of investors lost money as Northern Rock's share price plummeted, if you know how to read charts you would have identified the coming collapse of the share price and you could have made a profit by "selling short" the shares. Yes, you can make money even when the stock market is falling.

Figure 1.4

Chapter 2

Stock Market Basics

A really important hurdle to becoming a complete trader is learning to identify and accept your own limits. There are limits to how frequently you should trade, how much money you should place at risk, how many different stocks or commodities you should invest in, how many technical indicators you should use, and so on.

-Hank Pruden

What is the Objective of Investing in the Stock Market

Like any other business or investment, the main reason someone would get involved in the stock market is to make a profit. The conventional method is to buy shares at a particular price, and sell at a higher price. The difference between the price paid for the shares and the price they were sold represents the profit or loss made on the transaction.

What is a Share/Stock

Let's start by defining what a share is.

A share is a piece of ownership in a company. Buying shares in a company makes you a partial owner of that company. Collectively, the company is owned by all the shareholders, and each share represents a claim on assets and earnings. For example, Tesco is owned by shareholders with each shareholder owning a particular number of shares.

Throughout this book, the words shares and stocks will be used interchangeably. For the purpose of this book we would assume that they mean the same thing.

How are share prices quoted?

A quote consists of two prices, an offer to sell, called the ask price, and an offer to buy, called the bid price.

- **Ask**

  The ask price is the price a seller is willing to accept for a security, i.e. the amount you get when you sell your shares.

- **Bid**

  The price a buyer is willing to pay for a security, i.e. the price you pay when buying shares.

For example, if a share is quoted at 170/170.8; 170 is the ask price, i.e. the price at which the seller would be selling. While 170.8 is the bid price, i.e. the price the buyer will be paying for the share. In simpler terms, if you are buying the stock, you would be buying at 170.8, but if you own the stock and you want to sell, you would be selling it at 170.

How are Shares Valued?

Stock analysts use things such as P/E ratios, company growth, and a load of other figures to estimate current and future values of a company's share.

In reality, over the short term, the behaviour of the market (and share prices) is based on enthusiasm, sentiment, fear, rumours, and news. Over the long term, though, it is mainly company earnings that determine whether a stock's price will go up, down, or sideways.

The value of a share may go up or down depending on supply and demand for the stock. Generally share prices rise when more of the shares are being bought than sold and vice versa.

Bull and Bear Markets

There are 2 types of markets, a bull market and a bear market. Later on in this book we would mention a sideways market/trend. A sideways market happens within a bull market or a bear market. It is sometimes referred to as a consolidation period.

- **Bull Market**

  A bull market is in existence when the overall stock market is rising, i.e., in an upward trend.

- **Bear Market**

  A bear market is in existence when the overall stock market is falling, i.e., in a downward trend.

Markets and Indices

Shares and other financial instruments (currencies, commodities etc) are grouped into markets, exchanges and indexes. Shares are also organised into sectors and industries.

- **Stock Markets/Exchanges**

A stock exchange is an organisation where shares of stock and common stock equivalents are bought and sold. It is a marketplace where brokers and dealers meet to buy and sell stocks of publicly traded companies on behalf of investors. Examples include the London Stock Exchange (LSE) and the New York Stock Exchange (NYSE).

- **Stock Market Index**

A stock market index is a method of measuring a section of the stock market, e.g. the 100 largest companies, or transport companies.

Stock market indices are classed in many ways. A *broad-base* index represents the performance of a whole stock market. The most regularly quoted market indices are broad-base indices composed of the stocks of large companies listed on a nation's largest stock exchanges, such as the British FTSE 100, the French CAC 40, the German DAX, the Japanese Nikkei 225, the American Dow Jones Industrial Average and S&P 500 Index, and the Indian Sensex.

More specialised indices exist by tracking the performance of specific sectors of the market, e.g. the Dow Jones Transportation Index, Housing Index, etc.

What makes share prices move up or down?

The following factors can make share prices rise or fall;

- **The economy**
  The economy is usually in a state of boom or bust, expansion or contraction. The current state of an economy will have an impact on share prices. When the economy is expanding, share prices tend to rise. When the economy is contracting, share prices tend to fall. For instance, when a country is in a recession no stock is immune, irrespective of whether the fundamentals of the company are solid or if demand for the company's products is still high.

- **Market move**
  As mentioned earlier we are either in a bull market or a bear market. The stock market can be experiencing an uptrend as a result of the bull market, a downtrend as a result of the bear market, or it might be going sideways, i.e. consolidating. When the overall stock market is moving higher most company shares increase in value.

- **Sector move**
  Share prices also tend to follow the current trend within its sector. For instance, share prices of companies within the oil sector tend to rise, while share prices of companies within the transportation sector fall when the price of crude oil rises.

- **Earnings announcement**
  Companies announce their results on a regular basis. If the result that is announced is different from what market analysts are

expecting, it can lead to an immediate reaction on the share price. If you are new to trading you should not trade a company's stock just before the company makes an earnings announcement.

- **Broker upgrade/downgrade**
  Everyday around the world, market analyst express their opinions about particular companies. For instance, an analyst might say that considering the current market and the company's medium term goals they feel that the company's share price is undervalued and thereby upgrade the share. This could lead to the share price of that company moving higher. On the other hand, an analyst might say that a company is overvalued and downgrade the share. This could trigger a fall in the share price of the company.

- **Director buying/selling**
  By law when directors buy shares of their company they have to make it public knowledge. When directors are buying shares of their own company it is usually taken as an indication that the company is doing well and the share price is likely to rise. When directors sell shares, it can be an indication that the company might not be performing well and that the share price might fall in the near future.

A Trader versus an Investor

The terms trader and investor are used interchangeably in this book. Although some people would argue that anyone that holds a stock for a short period of time is a trader, I personally believe that since the end goal of the activity is to make a profit, the person that engages in buying and selling shares, or making money in the stock market is an investor. By definition, to invest means, to commit (money or capital) in order to gain a financial return. An investor is any party that makes an investment. An investment is an investment irrespective of the life time of the investment.

Trading is a term used to describe the act of buying and selling shares (or other financial instruments). When you buy or sell a share, you have placed a trade. The practice of buying and selling shares is called trading, the participants are called traders, and because the objective is to make a profit, they are also investors.

Time frames for trading

These timeframes are the length of time that investors/traders hold shares for.

- **Day Trading**

  This involves opening a position and closing it the same day. This style is used by professional and full time traders. It is not suitable for someone who has full time job or someone that just wants to use the stock market as an additional stream of income.

- **Swing Trading**

  Swing trading involves holding positions for anything between 2 days to 4 weeks. A trader or investor using this style would often use a combination of daily and weekly charts to perform their analysis.

- **Position Trading**

  Position trading involves holding a position for anything between 2 weeks to 6 months. A trader or investor using this style would often use daily, weekly, and monthly charts to perform their analysis. This style is used to build wealth. Profits gained using this style are usually reinvested or used to generate more profits. This style has proved to be very profitable because most stock market profits are not made by holding a stock for a day or 2 but are made by holding a stock over a longer term.

- **Long-Term Trading**

  Also referred to as **buy and hold** is when a stock is held for a long time, usually more than one year. A trader or investor using this style would also use weekly and monthly charts to perform their analysis.

This book is designed for swing, position and long term trading.

Chapter 3

What is Technical Analysis and why is it important?

"Investing without research is like playing stud poker and never looking at the cards."

- Peter Lynch

Stock analysts and investors use fundamental or technical analysis to determine the movement of share prices. While fundamental analysis involves analysing the financial health and future prospects of a company and using the results to predict the current or future value of the company's share price, technical analysis is the study of past and current price action of a share with the aim of identifying the trend of the share or any potential reversals in the current trend. This book explores technical analysis.

Technical analysts believe that the historical performance of stocks and markets are indications of future performance. Technical analysis is based on human psychology, and even though the stock market has been around for a long time, human psychology hardly changes.

Technical analysts do not attempt to measure a stock's real value, but instead they use charts and other tools to try and identify patterns that can suggest future activity of share prices. In the previous chapter I mentioned that over the short term, share prices are determined by enthusiasm, sentiment, fear, rumours, and news while over the long term it is determined mainly by the company earnings and other fundamentals. Technical analysts believe that all this information is presented in a graphical format (the chart) to assist investors in making decisions.

By studying price and volume changes, trends, and indicators used to track various components of market activity, a technical analyst hopes to make early identification of patterns and significant changes in supply and demand that allow for a forecast of prices to follow.

What is a trend?

In the stock market a trend is the direction in which the stock market or the share price of a company is moving. The key points to note about a trend are;

- Generally there is a continuance of the general trend until there is an opposing force that changes the trend.

- One of the key aspects of profitable trading is the early identification of trend reversals and to be able to develop a confidence level with regard to a continuation in the current trend in prices.

- One of the underlying principles in technical analysis is the identification of a trend and following the trend.

- There are 3 types of trends, uptrend, downtrend or sideways.

Stock Market Charts

In very simple terms, a stock market chart is a graphical representation of the movement of a share price over a period of time, e.g. 1 week, 1 month, 2 years etc.

The 3 most popular types of charts are;

- Line Chart
- Bar Chart
- Candlestick Chart

All three types of chart portray the same information but in different formats. The following 3 charts are for the same company. They are daily charts and represent the same time frame. I have included the charts so that you can visualise the differences between the ways information is presented by the 3 types of charts.

Line Chart

A line chart is plotted by drawing lines to connect the closing prices of a company's share price. Line charts don't show any of the price action that takes place during the day. This is the most basic type of chart, similar to the type that we learnt at school. An example is given below.

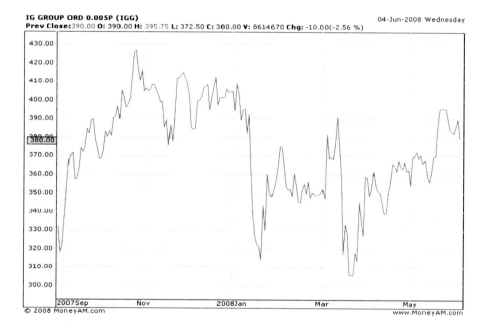

Figure 3.1

Bar Chart

On a bar chart each period, e.g. day is represented by a vertical line, with small horizontal lines on each side. The line on the left indicates the opening price(OP), while the line on the right indicates the closing price(CP).

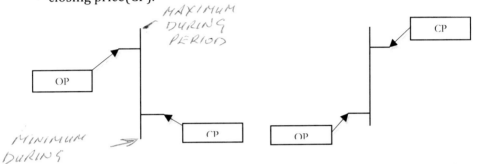

Figure 3.2 is an example of a bar chart.

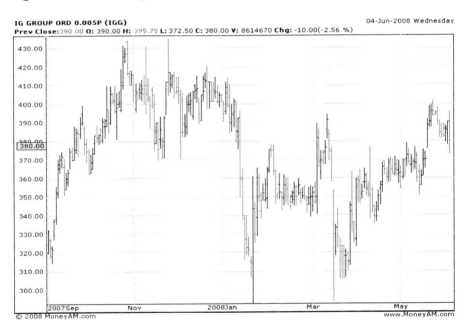

Figure 3.2

Candlestick Charts

A candlestick consists of a long vertical line, and a narrow horizontal line. Each candlestick includes the open, high, low, and close, of the timeframe, and also shows the direction (upward or downward), and the range of the timeframe. The following diagram illustrates a typical candlestick.

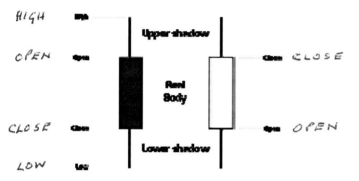

Figure 3.3 is an example of a candlestick chart.

Figure 3.3

Chapter 4

Introduction to Candlesticks

An investor's worst enemy is not the stock market but his own emotions.

Candlestick charting has become one of the most popular forms of stock market charting. Candlestick charts were developed in the 18th century by legendary Japanese rice trader Homma Munehisa. The charts gave Homma and others an overview of open, high, low, and close market prices over a certain period. This style of charting is very popular due to the level of ease in reading and understanding the graphs. Candlestick charts provide a fairly reliable tool to predict future movements in share prices. Candlesticks provide a visual view of the market sentiment. Candlestick charts was introduced to the west by Steve Nison.

Candlesticks are usually composed of the body (black or white), and an upper and a lower shadow. The shadows indicate the highest and lowest traded prices of a stock during the period represented. The body illustrates the opening and closing trades. If the stock closed higher than it opened, the body is white or unfilled, with the opening price at the bottom of the body and the closing price at the top. If the stock closed lower than it opened, the body is black, with the opening price at the top and the closing price at the bottom.

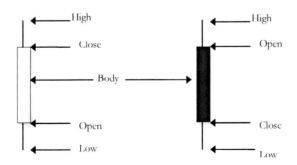

Some candlestick charts may replace the black or white of the candlestick body with colours such as red (for a lower closing) and blue or green (for a higher closing). Once you become familiar with the basic candlestick patterns you will quickly assimilate their meaning and easily interpret them.

It is important to note that candlesticks are simply a way of interpreting data on a chart. They should not be used in isolation but should be used in conjunction with some of the other technical indicators that we would discuss later.

Candlestick Patterns

On a candlestick chart a pattern is either a single candlestick formation or a combination of two or three candlestick formations that depict a potential change in the direction of a share price. Investors or traders that use candlesticks to determine whether to buy or sell would do so based on known candlestick patterns.

shall

There are a number of candlestick patterns, but we ~~would~~ only look at six patterns in this book. These six patterns are some of the most popular and reliable candlestick patterns.

Hammer

A hammer is a candlestick pattern that consists of a single candlestick. The candlestick has a small real body and a long lower shadow. Although technically the real body can either be white of black, from experience I have discovered that hammers with a white real body are more reliable. The diagrams below depict what a hammer looks like.

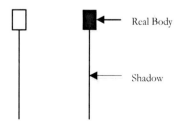

The long lower shadow indicates that the stock sold off sharply during the session and then bounced back to close near the sessions high. For the hammer to be effective, the stock must have been in a downtrend (It can be a short-term, medium-term or long-term downtrend). Three important characteristics of a hammer are;

- It must have no (or a very small, almost invisible) upper shadow.
- The lower shadow must take out the low of the previous session, i.e. the low of the session must be lower than the low of the previous session.
- The stock must be in a downtrend.

The chart below shows an example of a hammer and how the sentiment towards the stock changed after the appearance of the hammer.

Figure 4.1

The Shooting Star

The shooting star pattern is similar to the hammer. Its shape is like an inverted hammer. The candlestick has a small real body and a long upper shadow. Although technically the real body can either be white of black, from experience I have discovered that shooting star patterns with a black real body are more reliable. The diagrams below depict what a shooting star looks like.

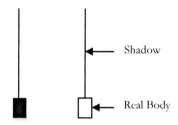

The long upper shadow shows that the stock rose sharply during the session and then fell to close near the sessions low. Three important characteristics of a shooting star are;

- It must have no (or a very small, almost invisible) lower shadow.
- The upper shadow must take out the high of the previous session, i.e. the high of the session must be higher than the high of the previous session.
- The stock must be in an uptrend (It can be a short-term, medium-term or long-term uptrend).

Figure 4.2 contains an example of a shooting star candlestick pattern. Take a look at the chart and study what happened after the appearance of the shooting star.

Shooting stars are one of the most reliable candlestick patterns. In most cases, a shooting star is accompanied by a fall in the share price of a stock.

Figure 4.2

Bullish Engulfing Pattern

The Bullish Engulfing pattern consists of two candlesticks. A bullish engulfing pattern is formed when a small black candlestick is followed by a large white candlestick that completely covers or "engulfs" the previous session's candlestick. The occurrence of a bullish engulfing pattern hints that the bulls have taken control of the share price movement from the bears. It suggests that a bottom or an end to a stock's decline might have taken place. The second candlestick opens lower than the previous candlestick's close, it then trades higher so by the end of the session, it will close above the previous candlestick's open.

The diagram below shows what a bullish engulfing pattern looks like.

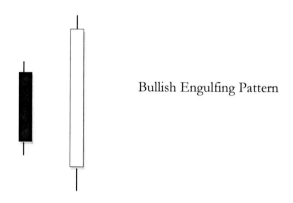

Bullish Engulfing Pattern

Figure 4.3 contains an example of a bullish engulfing pattern. The pattern was formed between the end of February and the beginning of March 2009. After the bullish engulfing pattern was formed, the share price of Blackstone Group LP rallied from around $4.75 to around $14 before it experienced another pullback. In most cases, bullish engulfing patterns signal a change in sentiment towards a stock. The rally following the pattern can either be a short term rally or a long term rally.

Figure 4.3

Bearish Engulfing Pattern

The bearish engulfing pattern is the opposite of the bullish engulfing pattern. It also consists of two candlesticks. A bearish engulfing pattern is formed when a small white candlestick is followed by a large black candlestick that completely covers or "engulfs" the previous session's candlestick. The occurrence of a bearish engulfing pattern hints that the bears have taken control of a stock's price movement from the bulls. It suggests that a top or an end to a stock's upward movement might have taken place. The second candlestick opens higher than the previous candlestick's close, it then trades lower and by the end of the session, it will close below the previous candlesticks' open.

The diagram below shows what a bearish engulfing pattern looks like.

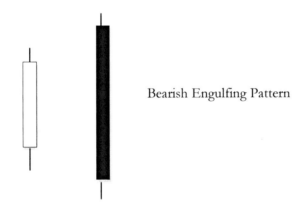

Bearish Engulfing Pattern

A bearish engulfing pattern has two important features;

- The black real body must wrap around (cover) the preceding white real body.
- The stock must be in an uptrend (short term, medium term or long term).

Figure 4.4 is a weekly chart of Red Hat, Inc. It contains an example of a bearish engulfing pattern. The pattern was formed in June 2008. After the bearish engulfing pattern was formed, the share price of

Red Hat, Inc fell from around $24.50 to around $8.50 before it experienced another major reversal. In most cases, bearish engulfing patterns signal a change in sentiment towards a stock. The fall in share prices following the pattern can either be short term or long term.

Figure 4.4

The Piercing Pattern

The piercing pattern is a bullish reversal pattern. It is made up of two candlesticks, the first one black, the second one white, both with fairly large bodies and small shadows. The second candlestick (i.e. white candlestick) must open below the first candlestick (i.e. black candlestick) and close at least half way up into the body of the black candlestick. A piercing pattern appears when the share price is in a downtrend. An important thing to note about a piercing pattern is that the greater the level of penetration into the black real body, the greater the likelihood of a reversal in the trend.

The diagram below shows what a piercing pattern looks like.

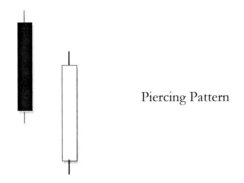

Piercing Pattern

A piercing pattern has three important features;

- The stock must be in a downtrend (short term, medium term or long term).
- The opening price of the second candlestick (i.e. the white candlestick) must be lower than the closing price of the first candlestick (i.e. the black candlestick).
- The white real body must close at least half way into prior session's black real body.

Figure 4.5 contains an example of a piercing pattern. The pattern was formed around the 22nd and 23rd of February 2009. Note that there was a short term rally in the share price after the appearance of the piercing pattern. In most cases, piercing patterns signal a change in sentiment towards a stock. The rally following the pattern can either be a short term rally or a long term rally.

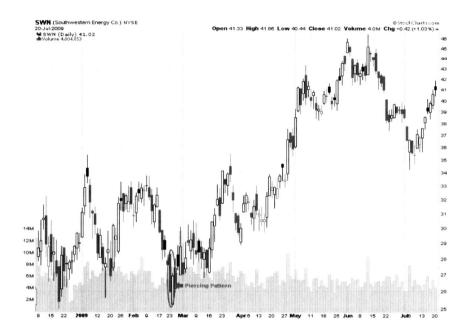

Figure 4.5

Dark Cloud Cover

The dark cloud cover is a bearish reversal pattern. It is the reverse of the piercing pattern. It is made up of two candlesticks, the first one is white, while the second one is black. Both candlesticks have fairly large bodies and small shadows. The second candlestick (i.e. black candlestick) must open above the first one (i.e. white candlestick) and close at least half way up into the body of the white candlestick. The dark cloud cover pattern appears when the share price is in an uptrend. It signals the possibility of a reversal in the upward trend. An important thing to note about the dark cloud cover is that the greater the level of penetration into the white real body, the greater the likelihood of a reversal in the trend.

The diagram below shows what a dark cloud cover looks like.

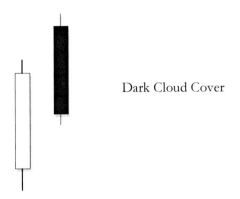

Dark Cloud Cover

A dark cloud cover pattern has three important features;

- The stock must be in an uptrend (short term, medium term or long term).
- The opening price of the second candlestick (i.e. the black candlestick) must be higher than the closing price of the first candlestick (i.e. the white candlestick).
- The black real body must close at least half way into prior session's white real body.

Figure 4.6 is a daily chart of Land Securities. It contains an example of a Dark Cloud pattern. The pattern was formed in February 2009. After the dark cloud cover pattern was formed, the share price of Land Securities fell from around 700p to around 360p before it witnessed another major upside reversal. In most cases, dark cloud cover patterns signal a change in sentiment towards a stock. It indicates that the recent sell-off in the particular stock has been exhausted and bulls are about to take over from the bears. The fall in share prices following the pattern can either be short term or long term.

Figure 4.6

Chapter 5

Charting Basics

"I never buy anything unless I can fill out on a piece of paper my reasons. I may be wrong, but I would know the answer to that. "I'm paying $32 billion today for the Coca Cola Company because..." If you can't answer that question, you shouldn't buy it. If you can answer that question, and you do it a few times, you'll make a lot of money."

- Warren Buffet

Things get more technical from this chapter. Let's start with the basics of charting.

Support and Resistance

Support and resistance are two very important features of technical analysis. Support refers to prices or levels on a chart that tend to act as a floor by preventing the price of a share from falling further. Resistance is regarded as a ceiling because they are price levels that a stock would have difficulty rising above.

When the share price is finally able to break out and go above an identified resistance level, or fall below an identified support, the previous level of support changes its role and become a new area of resistance and a resistance level become a new support level.

Figure 5.1 contains an example of a typical support and resistance scenario. Take a close look at the left hand side of the chart and you'll notice that as the share price of Sprint Nextel Corp. fell from $8, it continued falling until it found support at around $3. The share price bounced off this level twice between October and November 2008. The share price finally broke through the support level around the 11th of November, after which it continued its downward trend. You'll also notice that this level of support became a resistance level when the share price began its upward trend.

Figure 5.1

Gaps

A gap is formed on a chart when the opening price of a share is much different than the previous day's closing price. The key points to note about gaps are;

- A price gap can be to the upside or to the downside, i.e. the share might open much higher or much lower than the previous day's closing price.
- A price gap generally takes place just before a significant price pattern.
- Sometimes after the gap has occurred, the share price begins to stay within a range before continuing in the direction of the gap.
- Gaps are not visible on line charts.

The following two charts give examples of gaps on a chart.

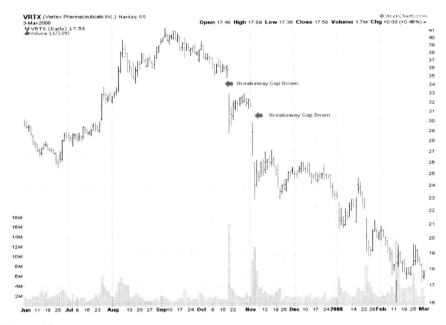

Figure 5.2

In figure 5.2, a downside breakaway gap occurred in October 2007. The gap signalled the beginning of another downtrend in the stock. After the breakaway gap on the chart, Vertex Pharmaceuticals Inc's share price dropped from around $33 to $17 over a period of 5 months.

In figure 5.3, two downside breakaway gaps occurred, both in January 2008. The gaps show the weakness in the share price. It also shows that there is a very high probability that the share price would continue to fall. Intel's share price fell by around $8 over a period of 3 months.

Figure 5.3

Double Top and Double Bottom

A double top is a chart pattern which occurs when a share price rises to a particular level, drops back from that level, then makes a second run to that level, and then finally drops back off again. It is a reversal pattern.

A double bottom occurs when a share price drops to a particular level, and then rises back from that level, then makes a second drop to that level, and then finally rises up from that level again. It is also a reversal pattern.

Figure 5.4 contains an example of a double top and a double bottom.

Figure 5.4

Chapter 6

Moving Average (MA)

What beat me was not having brains enough to stick to my own game – that is, to play the market only when I was satisfied that precedents favoured my play. There is the plain fool, who does the wrong thing at all times everywhere, but there is also the Wall Street fool, who thinks he must trade all the time. No man can have adequate reasons for buying or selling stocks daily – or sufficient knowledge to make his play an intelligent play.

- Jesse Livermore

It's almost impossible to talk about technical analysis without mentioning moving average.

The following points contain the main things that you need to know about moving averages;

- A moving average is plotted alongside a price chart.
- A moving average shows the average value of a share's price over a set period, e.g. 20 days. For instance, a 5 day moving average will be calculated as (P1+P2+P3+P4+P5)/5, where P1 is the closing price of the stock on day 1, i.e. the addition of the closing prices over 5 working days and divided by 5.
- Moving averages are generally used to measure momentum and define areas of possible support and resistance.
- Moving averages are used to emphasis the direction of a trend and to smooth out price and volume fluctuations, or "noise" on a chart. When the moving average is heading down, this indicates that the stock is in a downtrend, when the moving average is heading up the stock is in an uptrend.
- Typically an upward movement in a stock is confirmed when a short term moving average (e.g.15-day) crosses above a longer term average (e.g. 50-day). Downward movement is confirmed when a short term moving average crosses below a long term average.

The following chart shows a 20 day moving average plotted along-side the share price. You would notice that the moving average is smoother than the price chart and it shows the trend of the share price without all the "noise".

Figure 6.1

The 2 most popular types of moving averages are

- Simple Moving Average
- Exponential Moving Average

Simple Moving Average (SMA)

A simple moving average is calculated by adding the closing price of the security for a number of time periods and then dividing this total by the number of time periods. For example, a 10 day moving average is calculated by adding the closing prices of each of the 10 days and dividing the total by 10.

In a simple moving average all days (or periods) have the same weighting.

Short-term averages respond quickly to changes in the price of the underlying stock, while long-term averages are slow to react. For example, a 5 day moving average would respond faster to changes in a share price compared to a 10 day moving average.

Exponential Moving Average (EMA)

The exponential moving average is similar to a simple moving average, except that more weight is given to the most recent data. For example, in a 10 day moving average day 10 (the most recent day) has a higher weighting than day 1 (the oldest day).

This type of moving average reacts faster to recent price changes than a simple moving average. The 12-day and 26-day EMAs are the most popular short-term averages, and they are used to create indicators like the moving average convergence divergence (MACD).

How to use Moving Averages to make decisions

Moving averages can be used in 3 ways;

- To identify or confirm a trend.
- To identify or confirm support and resistance levels
- To identify trend reversals via moving average crossover signals

Identifying and Confirming the Trend

The moving average can be used to identify and confirm the current trend of a stock. As mentioned earlier, when the slope of the moving average is heading down, this indicates that the stock is in a downtrend, when slope of the moving average is heading up the stock is in an uptrend.

In figure 6.2 the moving averages confirm that Persimmon was in a downtrend at the time the chart was taken.

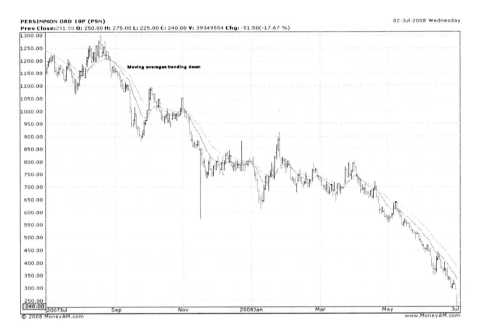

Figure 6.2

Using Moving Averages as Support and Resistance Levels

Moving averages can also be used to identify support and resistance levels. In figure 6.3, the 20 day MA served as resistance between August and September. When studying charts it is vital that you keep a close look on the moving average just in case it acts as support or resistance.

Figure 6.3

Identifying Trend Reversals through Moving Average Crossover Signals

Moving averages also generate signals when they cross each other, or when they cross the price. When a faster moving average crosses a slower moving average while heading up, the point at which they crossed is a buy signal. If the faster moving average crosses the slower moving average heading down, the point at which they crossed is a sell signal.

In September 2007 in figure 6.4, the 13 day exponential moving average (the fast MA) crossed the 26 day exponential moving average (the slow MA). That produced a buy signal, i.e. it is okay to buy the stock at that point. After that point there was a short term rally in the share price. A sell signal was produced in November of the same year.

Figure 6.4

Figure 6.5

Similarly in figure 6.5, buy and sell signals were given at points where the moving averages crossed around the end of January and the end of July, respectively.

Chapter 7

Moving Average Convergence Divergence (MACD)

"The professional concerns himself with doing the right thing rather than making money, knowing that the profit takes care of itself if the other things are attended to."

- Jesse Livermore

Moving Average Convergence Divergence (MACD) is one of the simplest and most reliable indicators available. The indicator was developed by Gerald Appel. The MACD uses moving averages which are lagging indicators to calculate the trend of an instrument. To draw the MACD, the longer moving average is deducted from the shorter moving average. The result forms a line that oscillates above and below zero, without any upper or lower limits. Does it sound too technical? Don't worry, most technical analysis software will compute this for you so you won't need to worry about how this is calculated.

The most popular parameters for MACD are 26, 12 and 9. 26 and 12 are the moving averages used for the computation while 9 is the parameter used to generate the histogram lines. The MACD can be displayed at the top or the bottom of a chart. Technical Analysts can adjust these numbers to come up with a MACD that is best suited for different securities or different trading personalities.

The MACD generates both buy and sell signals. We will look at two ways in which signals are generated by the MACD.

1. Moving Average Crossovers
2. Centreline Crossovers

MACD Moving Average Crossover

A Moving Average Crossover on the MACD may produce either a buy (bullish) signal or a sell (bearish) signal.

Bullish Moving Average Crossover

A buy signal is generated when the faster moving average crosses the slower moving average heading up, e.g., when the 12 period moving average crosses the 26 period moving average heading up.

In figure 7.1, there are 3 instances where the moving averages cross to generate buy signals. The most recent one on the chart occurred around the 11th of February 2008. The entry level was around $78. The share price of the stock then increased by around 10% before generating a sell signal. If you want to buy a stock based on this signal it is extremely important that you wait till the moving averages crossover. Your ability to stay put till the moving averages cross is vital and it will reduce the number of errors that you make.

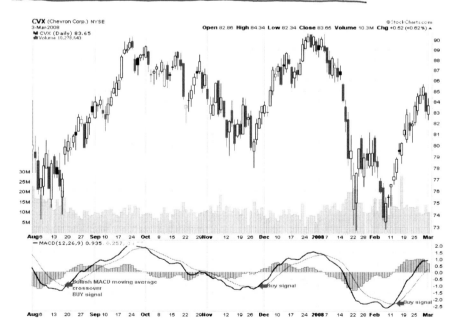

Figure 7.1

As you become more experienced you would notice that there would be many instances where the moving averages will contract, appear as if they are about to crossover, but would not.

Remember, it is important to wait for the crossover to take place before you take action. You buy the stock after the crossover has taken place.

In figure 7.2 there are 4 instances of a bullish moving average crossover on the MACD.

Figure 7.2

Bearish Moving Average Crossover

A sell signal is generated when the faster moving average crosses the slower moving average heading down, e.g., when the 12 period moving average crosses the 26 period moving average heading down.

If you already own a stock, a sell signal can be an indication to sell and close that position. Figure 7.3 shows the corresponding sell signals for the buy signals shown on figure 7.1.

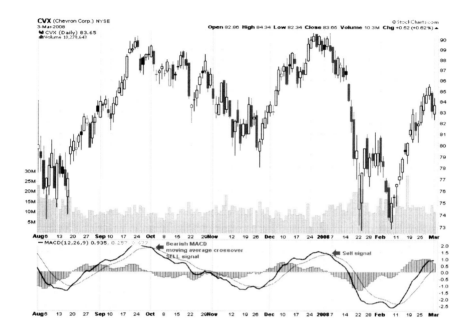

Figure 7.3

Take a look at figure 7.4 and take note of what happened after the bearish moving average crossovers on the MACD.

Also take a look at figure 7.5 and identify the points where there is a bearish moving average crossover. What action would you have taken at the points where the moving averages crossed and why?

Figure 7.4

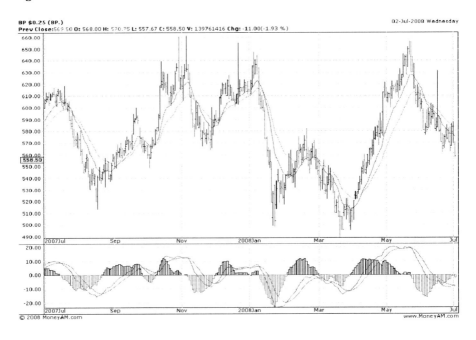

Figure 7.5

Now take a look at figure 7.6 and identify the points where there is a bearish MACD moving average crossover. What action would you have taken at the points where the moving averages crossed and why?

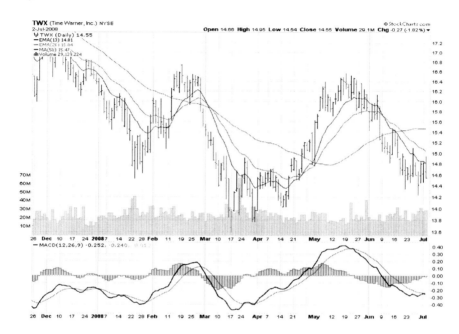

Figure 7.6

MACD Centreline Crossover

A MACD centreline crossover occurs when the MACD histogram lines move from above the zero line to below it, or from below the zero line to above it.

Bullish Centreline Crossover

- A Bullish Centreline Crossover occurs when MACD moves above zero and into positive territory.

55

- This is an indication that momentum has changed from negative to positive or from bearish to bullish.

- The centreline crossover can be used as an independent signal, or to confirm other signals such as a moving average crossover. Once MACD crosses into positive territory, momentum, at least for the short term, has turned bullish.

- Figure 7.7 contains 3 examples of a bullish MACD centreline crossover.

- A bullish centreline crossover signifies that it is okay to buy the stock.

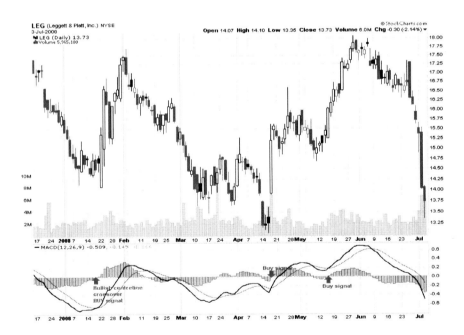

Figure 7.7

Bearish Centreline Crossover

- A Bearish Centreline Crossover occurs when MACD moves below zero and into negative territory.

- This is an indication that momentum has changed from positive to negative or from bullish to bearish. A bearish centreline crossover signifies that it might be time to sell the stock if you currently own it.

- The centreline crossover can be used as an independent signal, or to confirm other signals such as a moving average crossover. Once MACD crosses into negative territory, momentum, at least for the short term, has turned bearish.

- Figure 7.8 contains 2 examples of a bearish MACD centreline crossover.

Figure 7.8

To increase your chances of success when using the MACD, here are four things you should note and try to avoid especially if you are new to trading or if you trade part time;

(1) Don't buy a stock if the moving averages on the MACD chart are heading down

(2) Don't sell short if the moving averages on the MACD chart are heading up

(3) Don't buy a stock (or do so with extreme caution) if the MACD lines are below midline.

(4) Don't sell short (or do so with extreme caution) if the MACD lines are above midline.

Chapter 8

Relative Strength Index (RSI)

"Be Patient, Be deliberate. Wait for the perfect setup. When you see it don't hesitate. If it's not happening, don't take action"

- Entries & Exits

The Relative Strength Index (RSI) indicator was developed by J. Welles Wilder. RSI compares the magnitude of a stock's recent gains to the magnitude of its recent losses and turns that information into a number that ranges between 0 and 100. To arrive at the number, it uses a single parameter called the number of periods. In his book, Wilder recommended using 14 periods.

The RSI generates 3 types of signals

- Overbought/Oversold
- Centreline Crossovers
- Divergences

WILL
We ~~would~~ only discuss the first 2 signals in this book.

Overbought/Oversold signals

Wilder recommended using 70 and 30 as overbought and oversold levels. If the RSI rises above 30 it is considered bullish for the stock. Also, if the RSI falls below 70, it is considered a bearish signal. It is important to note that for the RSI indicator to be considered bullish, it must be rising from below 30. If the RSI drops below 30 and stays below 30, it is a sign that the stock is "out of favour" with investors and the share price might continue to fall. Likewise to be considered bearish it must be falling from above 70.

In the next chart of Stone Energy Corp (figure 8.1), the RSI dropped below 30 at the beginning of February 2009. However, as RSI stayed below 30, the share price continued to fall. The share price started to rise when RSI moved upward from below 30.

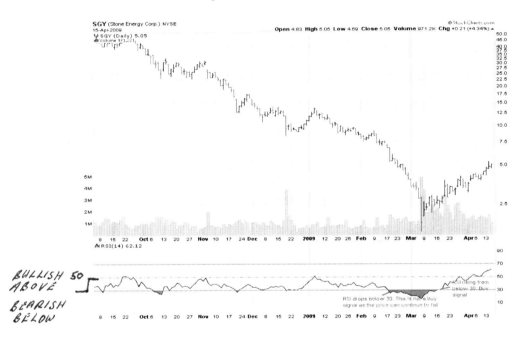

Figure 8.1

Centreline Crossover

The centreline for the RSI is 50. Readings above and below the centreline will indicate either a bullish or bearish sentiment. If the RSI is above 50, this stipulates that average gains in the share price are higher than average losses. If the RSI is below 50, it stipulates that the average losses in the share price are greater than the average gains. Some investors use a move above the centreline to confirm a bullish move or a move below 50 to confirm a bearish move.

Study figure 8.2 and take note of what happened at the points where RSI crossed 50, either going up or while coming down.

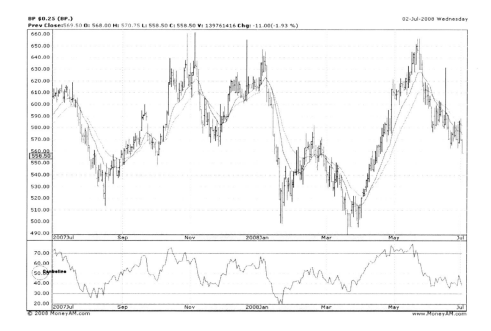

Figure 8.2

In the next chart (figure 8.3), the RSI crossed midline in March 2008, from that point the share price of Haliburton began a rally. A buy signal was produced when the RSI crossed midline (i.e. 50). Some investors would hold onto a stock as long as the RSI stays above 50. Note how share prices tend to drop when RSI is below 50 and trending down, and how they tend to rise when RSI is above 50 and trending up.

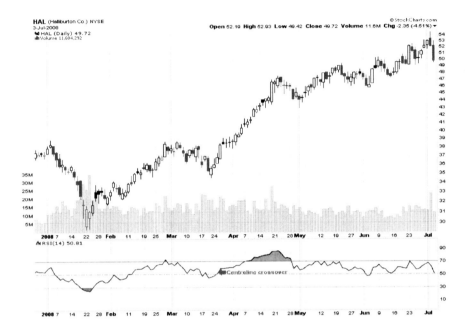

Figure 8.3

One last note on RSI.....

It's important not to get too wrapped up about overbought/oversold signals on the RSI. RSI can fall below 30 and stay below 30 for a long period, in fact the speed at which stocks fall when RSI is below 30 is much faster than the speed at which they fall when RSI is above 30. If you identify a stock whose RSI is below 30, you have to wait for the RSI to rise above 30 before you even consider buying the stock.

Similarly, an RSI above 70 does not necessarily mean that the share price of a stock will start to fall. In fact, when RSI is above 70 prices tend to rise at a very fast pace. Weakness in the stock kicks in when RSI falls below 70.

Chapter 9

Stochastics

"Don't move unless it is advantageous, do not execute unless it is effective, do not challenge unless it is critical"

- Sun Tzu in The Art of War

This indicator was developed by George C Lane in the late 1950's. It is a technical momentum indicator that compares a stock's closing price to its price range over a given time period. The indicator's sensitivity to market movements can be reduced by adjusting the time period. The indicator produces a value that is between 0 and 100. When it is plotted, it is two lines that move within a range of 0 and 100. The dotted line is called the %D which is a moving average of the smooth line, called the %K. These lines are generated by the charting software so you don't need to worry about the technical details.

When Stochastics is below 20 the stock is considered to be oversold, and if it is above 80 it is considered to be overbought. It's important to note that when Lane developed the indicator, he stressed that a reading below 20 was not necessarily bullish. Likewise a reading above 80 was not necessarily bearish. A stock can continue to rise after the stochastic indicator has reached 80 and it can continue to fall after the indicator has reached 20. Some of the best signals are derived when the indicator moves from above 80 back to below 80, and from below 20 back to above 20.

Buy and sell signals are also derived when %K crosses above or below %D. The %K and %D lines are shown on a chart.

In the next chart, instances where %K crossed above %D are marked "Buy signal" and instances where %K crosses below %D are marked "Sell signal".

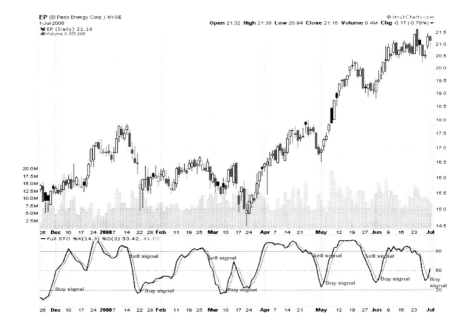

Figure 9.1

You'll notice that in figure 9.1 there are quite a few buy and sell signals. An investor or a trader that is only using the stock market as an additional source of income would not be able to trade all the signals so would need to combine these signals with other signals to determine whether the signals are strong enough to trade.

Figures 9.2 and 9.3 illustrate an example of using Stochastics to predict the next movement of a share price. On the 15th of February, the stochastic indicator on the Walt Disney chart is showing that the stock was overbought. The indicator is moving from above 80 back to below 80. Note that after the first chart was taken, you shouldn't rush and issue a sell instruction on the stock. You should the stock on your daily watch list and issue your sell instruction as soon as the indicator crosses below 80.

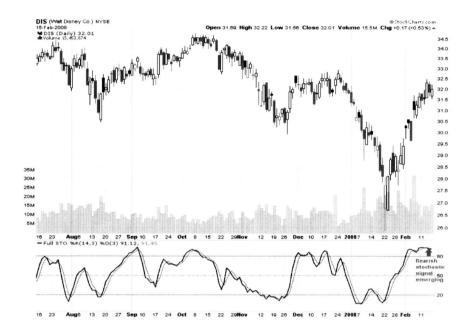

Figure 9.2

Looking at figure 9.3, you'll notice that the indicator crossed below 80 around the 26th of February. That is when you should issue your sell instruction.

It's important to remember that when you are using Stochastics as a sell signal, a reading above 80 does not necessarily mean that the share price is about to fall. The stochastic reading can stay above 80 for a long period. The sell signal is when the stochastic reading falls below 80 and is heading down.

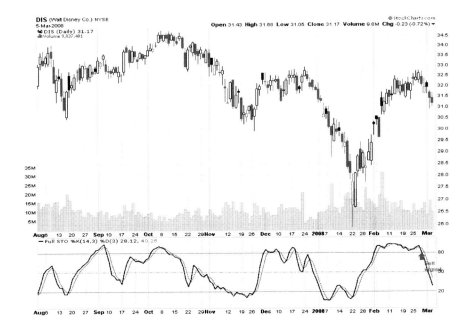

Figure 9.3

Chapter 10

Combining Multiple Indicators

"A man must believe in himself and his judgement if he expects to make a living at this game. "

-Jesse Livermore

None of the strategies or indicators we have looked at is foolproof. In this chapter we are going to look at how we can combine more than one indicator for consistent profits.

To reduce the probability of making a wrong decision, it is best to use more than one indicator to make a decision on whether to buy or sell a stock. For instance, when looking at a chart it is possible that the MACD indicator can give you a buy signal, while the Stochastics indicator gives a sell signal on the same chart. If that happens the best thing to do is not to take any action and let that transaction pass. It simply says that your indicators are out of sync, and it reduces your probability of making the right decision. On the other hand, if you combine 3 indicators and 2 out of 3, or all 3 indicators give you the same signal, it means all your indicators are in sync and the probability that you would make the right decision is very high. Personally I wouldn't place a trade based on a signal from a single indicator. If one of your indictors has given a buy signal and you expect others to do the same, you can put that stock on your watch list and start to monitor it.

In the chart below, all 3 indicators gave a combined buy signal around the 20th of August 2007, the 26th of November 2007 and the 11th of February 2008.

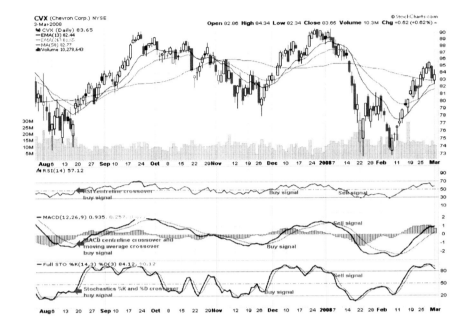

Figure 10.1

In the next chart (figure 10.2), all three indicators gave a combined buy signal around the 28th of January and a combined sell signal around the 26th of February. On the 28th of January the MACD crosses above midline. This signal is supported by the RSI which is rising up from 30 and the Stochastics indicator which had already given a buy signal. In the same chart, all three indicators gave sell signals during the first week in March 2008.

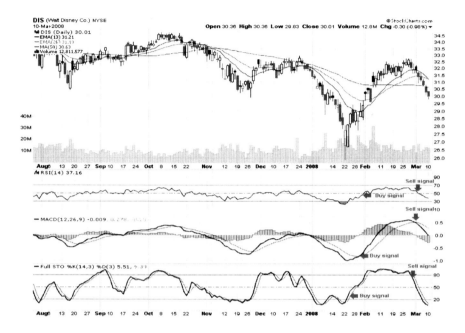

Figure 10.2

In figure 10.3, all 3 indicators gave a combined buy signal around the 26th of January and a combined sell signal around the end of February. MACD crossed above midline, RSI was rising up from 30, and stochastic was also giving a buy signal. If the stock was bought based on these signals, the position could have remained opened until the indicators gave a sell signal around the 27th of March.

If you are using multiple indicators to make a decision, it's best not to take any action if one of the indicators give a conflicting signal, e.g. if the MACD gives a buy signal but the Stochastic indicator gives a sell signal, do not touch that stock. If you are using 3 indicators, make sure that all indicators are giving the same signal. If you are using 2 indicators, make sure that both indicators are giving the same signal.

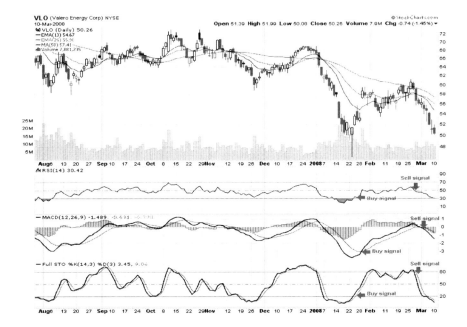

Figure 10.3

When combining the stochastic indicator with the MACD and the RSI, you'll notice that in most cases the stochastic would give a signal before the others, it's up to you to decide if you want to wait for the other indicators to give a signal. One of the advantages of waiting for the other indicators is that it reduces the probability of buying or selling based on weak/false signals.

When do you exit a position?

The moment you buy a stock, you need to have a documented plan on when you would exit the position. You would have to think about two types of exits. First you have to decide on the price at which you would exit the position if the trade does not go your way, i.e. let's assume you bought a stock and instead of rising, the price of the stock falls. You have to decide on the maximum that you are willing to lose. The price at which you decide to exit is called your stop. An order that closes a position if the price of your stock gets to that level is called a stop loss order. A stop loss order should be placed at the same time you open your position.

Second, you must also decide on how to exit a position with profits. It's been pointed out that share prices move in cycles. If you have a position that is in profit, you would ideally want to close it before it turns into a loss. To exit with a profit you can either set a target price when you enter a position, or you can monitor your indicators and close the position when your indicators show a potential reverse in the current trend.

Chapter 11

Weekly and Monthly Charts – For the medium to long term investor

True investors realize that 'get rich quick' usually means 'get poor quicker'

-Anonymous

This book has been designed mainly for people that would not have the time or opportunity to check their charts or positions every day. It's been designed on the assumption that the reader might only be able to review charts once or twice a week. If you fall into the category of people that cannot review charts every day due to time restrictions, I'll like to encourage you to pay particular attention to this chapter as it focuses on weekly and monthly charts.

One of the main advantages of using longer term charts is that it cuts out a lot of the "noise" and daily fluctuations that appear on daily charts. If you are using longer term charts, it's important that you do not get carried away by the daily fluctuations in prices. You have to determine the trend of the period you are using and stay in the position until the trend changes.

Most weekly or monthly charts that you would come across would either be a candlestick chart or a bar chart. On a weekly chart each period (candle or bar) represents one week, while on a monthly chart each period represents one month.

Using Weekly Charts

Weekly charts show the intermediate trend of a stock. Trends on a weekly chart tend to last a lot longer than trends on a daily chart however a trader has to be extremely disciplined to be able to sit through the trend. Weekly charts are a very important tool for the short term investor.

The chart below is a weekly chart of Sprint Nextel Corp. In January 2009 the MACD crossed above midline. This was supported with a rising RSI and a bullish crossover on the stochastic indicator. The combinations of these 3 signals give a very strong buy signal.

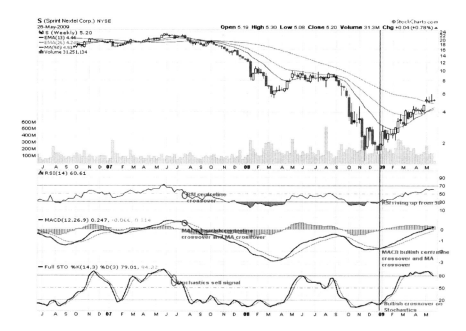

Figure 11.1

The best time to check the weekly charts is on weekends. This is because a period (a candlestick or a bar) on the weekly charts run from the first working day of the week through to the last working day of the week, usually Monday through to Friday, excluding bank (public) holidays. Signals are usually formed on completion of a period.

If you see a buy signal on the weekly chart, you can set an order to buy just above the highest price of the previous week, or wait till the market closes the following Monday and set an order to buy just above Monday's high.

Using Monthly Charts

Monthly charts provide a more realistic picture of the direction of a share price. Monthly charts do not give as many signals as daily or weekly charts, but the signals produced by a monthly chart are more reliable, i.e. monthly charts produce much less false signals than daily and weekly charts. Monthly charts are more suitable for the part time trader or investor. Shares bought based on signals from a monthly chart should normally be held for 3 months onwards. You need to realise that your big profits will not be made by trying to catch the daily fluctuations in price, but in identifying the medium to long term trend and riding the trend.

Technical indicators on monthly charts are read the same way they are read on charts representing shorter timeframes.

Figure 11.2

The above chart is a monthly chart of Gencorp Inc. The chart also contains the MACD and RSI indicators. On the chart there are fewer MACD crossovers than you would have on a chart of a shorter time frame. However, the signals when given have a higher probability of returning a profit to the investor as the trends last longer on a monthly chart. Also note that when the RSI is above 50, the share price is most likely to be rising. When RSI drops below 50, it signals a change in direction of the medium to long term trend. Having MACD above midline and RSI greater than 50 is an ideal combination to have on a monthly chart.

In the diagram below in April 2007 the MACD indicator fell below midline, coupled with a bearish MACD moving average crossover. Around the same period the RSI dropped below 50 and that signalled the beginning of a downward trend for OfficeMax Inc. This shows the power of using the 2 indicators to derive a signal from the monthly charts.

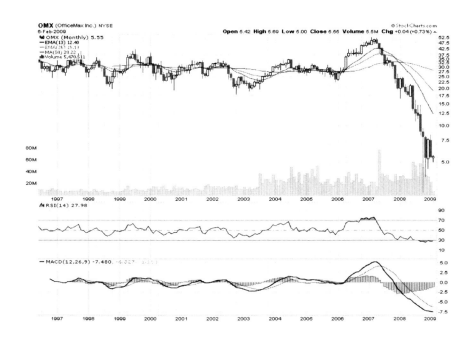

Figure 11.3

The following chart (figure 11.4) shows a couple of instances where the combination of the MACD and RSI indicators gave trading signals that would have been very profitable if executed correctly.

Figure 11.4

Figures 11.5 and 11.6 illustrate how you can use the monthly chart to enter a position. The first chart is a monthly chart of Advanced Micro Devices. The chart shows that medium to long term sentiment on the stock has turned bullish. MACD has risen above midline, RSI is rising up from 30 and stochastic is also rising up from 20.

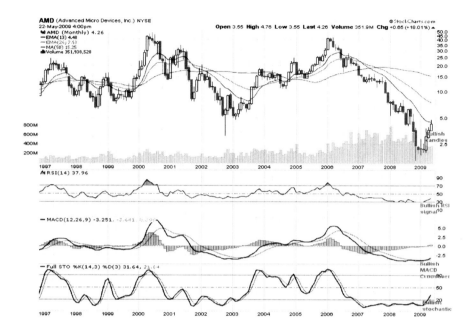

Figure 11.5

Even though the monthly chart is bullish and it signals the possibility of the stock rising over the medium to long term. Your goal as an investor should be to buy at the right time. To ensure you are buying at the right time you would also have to check the daily charts, to make sure that the signals are indicating buy. The next chart is the daily chart of Advanced Micro Devices. The indicators on the daily chart are showing that it is not the best time to buy stock. Since we are interested in the medium to long term, it does not mean that we would no longer consider buying it. You should put the stock on your watch list and monitor it every other day, after the stock market has closed. When indicators on the daily chart gives a buy signal, you should determine your entry level and issue the buy order.

Figure 11.6

Using candlestick charting with monthly charts

Candlesticks patterns on a monthly chart are more reliable and often give an early indication of a change in the direction or the trend of a stock. The trustworthiness of the signals is derived from the fact that the patterns take a longer period to form. It is generally useful to look out for hammers, spinning tops and engulfing patterns. It should also be noted that a monthly candlestick pattern is only completely formed at the end of a month. That means if you are looking at a monthly candlestick chart on the 15th of March, you should not take the candlestick that represents March as a pattern, because it is not completely formed. In this example, the candlestick representing March does not become a fully formed pattern until the 31st (or the last working day) of March.

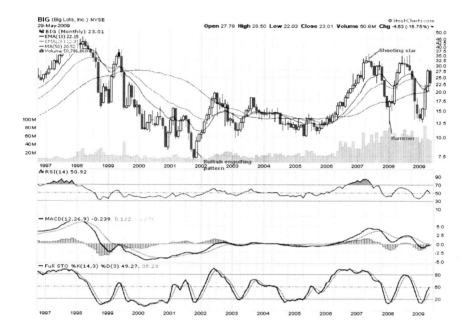

Figure 11.7

In figure 11.7 a bullish engulfing pattern formed in November 2001 signalling the beginning of an uptrend that lasted for about eight months. After the appearance of the pattern the stock rose from $10 to around $20. Another bullish engulfing pattern appeared in February 2009. Also on the chart, a hammer candlestick was formed on the chart in January 2008. This candlestick was followed by a rise in the share price that lasted for about five months. During the 5 month period the share price rose from $15 to around $35. The candlesticks on the chart provide an indication of the strength of candlesticks on a monthly chart.

In figure 11.8 a bullish engulfing pattern was formed in March 2003, after which the stock rallied from $10 to around $190 within six years.

Figure 11.8

Using the monthly chart to determine the trend of the overall stock market

As I write (April 2009), we have been in a bear market since 2007. In March 2009 a hammer was formed on the S&P 500 and FTSE 100 monthly charts (figures 11.9 and 11.10). This pattern indicates the possibility of the bear market having reached the bottom and a potential reversal in the trend of the market. The low of the hammer also represent support levels as it is unlikely that the market would drop below those levels in the short term.

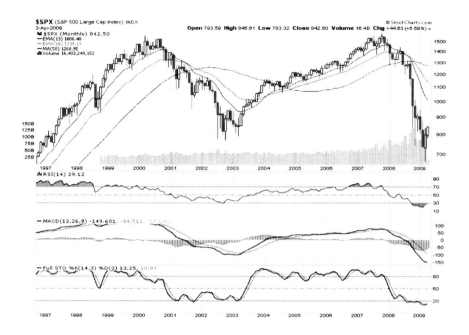

Figure 11.9

Figure 11.10

The Deji Odusi Wealth Building Methodology (TradVestor)

Daily charts might not be suitable for everyone, especially people that have a full time job and are using the stock market as an additional source of income, or just to build wealth. If you are not a full time trader, you would find using monthly charts a lot easier to use and a lot less time consuming. If used properly, monthly charts give reliable and profitable signals and it cuts out a lot of the fluctuations that appear on a daily chart.

What I have dubbed The Deji Odusi Wealth Building Methodology entails using monthly charts and three indicators, the MACD, the RSI and the stochastic indicator.

When scanning for stocks to buy, look for the following conditions on the chart:

- On the MACD indicator, the MACD must be above midline
- On the MACD indicator, the faster moving average (e.g. 13) must be above the slower moving average and they must both be rising.
- On the RSI indicator, the RSI must be greater than 30 and the slope of the RSI must be heading up.
- The stochastic must be above 20 and heading up.

If the above conditions are met, to enter a position;

(1) Make sure that the previous month closed higher than the month before it. For instance, if we are in March, ensure that the closing price of the stock at the end of February was higher than its closing price at the end of January.

(2) Take a note of the highest price of the day prior to your analysis. For instance if you are studying the chart on the 5th of May, take a note of the highest price the stock traded on the 4th of May.

(3) Place a stop order to buy the stock if it reaches the high of the previous day. Using our example of the 4th and 5th of May,

let's say that you want to buy XYZ, if the highest price the stock traded at on the 4th of May was $12.50, but it is now trading at $12.35, place a stop order to buy it at $12.53 (i.e. above the previous high of $12.50)

Taking the stress out of investing.

Monthly charts take a lot of stress out of investing if you use them properly. Just as moving averages cut out the 'noise' on a chart and smoothen the trend of a stock, monthly charts cut out the 'noise' and fluctuations that are evident on daily charts. Take a close look at the following 2 charts and observe how the daily chart gives sell signals, only to reverse after a while and continue the upward trend.

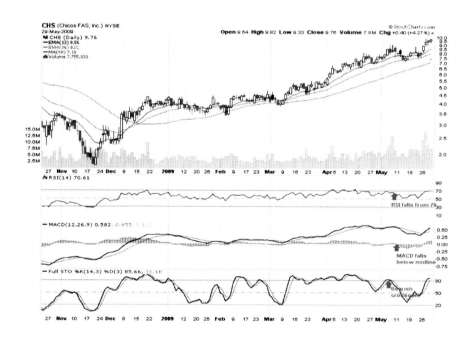

Figure 11.11

However, looking at the monthly chart you'll see that the stock in an uptrend which has just began. You'll also notice that all the fluctuations and signals that appear on the daily chart are not evident on the monthly chart. The sell signal that appeared on daily chart was just a pullback and not a reversal in the upward trend of the stock.

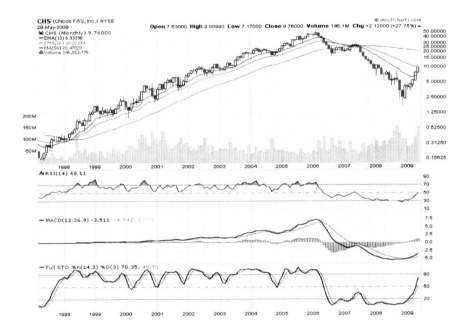

Figure 11.12

If you had bought Chicos FAS based on the signals from the monthly chart, the best way to manage the position is to wait for a reversal signal to appear on the monthly chart before selling. If you looked at the daily chart and sold your shares because of the sell signal on the daily chart, you would have sold your shares only to see the stock turn around and continue its upward trend.

To create wealth using monthly charts you have to be disciplined enough to hold your shares through the fluctuations that appear on daily charts.

Chapter 12

Placing Orders and Managing Your Positions

After analysing your charts and deciding whether to buy or sell a stock, the next step is to place your order with your broker. When you place your order to buy or sell a stock, you do not necessarily have to do so at the current market price, i.e. the price that the broker quotes for you. You can specify the price at which you want to buy or sell. If you decide to buy or sell at a price that is different from the current market price, your broker will put the order on his system and your order will be executed only if the price gets to the level that you specify. This is very handy for traders or investors that trade part time or cannot sit down in front of the computer all day.

Types of Orders

- **Market Order**

  A market order is the most common type of order. It is when you buy or sell at the current price that the broker quotes. For example, if I call my broker and ask for the current price of Cadbury's plc, if I decide to deal at the price that he quotes (e.g. 523/524), then I have placed a market order. Similarly, if I am dealing online, if I decide to buy or sell at the current displayed price, my order would be classified as a market order.

- **Buy Stop Order**

  A buy stop order is an order to buy a stock at a price that is higher than the price that is currently being quoted. For example, if I want to buy BP at 430, but it is currently being quoted as 425/425.5, I can leave an order to buy BP when the price reaches 430. A buy stop order is useful if you want to buy at a higher price to make sure that the stock price is really rising, for instance, you might want a stock to take out a previous day's high before buying. A buy stop order allows you to confirm the validity of a trend. If you use buy stop orders, there is a possibility that some of your orders will not get executed. Using my example, if BP rises to 428 and then reverses and starts to drop, my order will not be executed because BP did not trade at 430. If this happens don't fret, it just means that you have saved yourself from being in a losing position.

You can also place a buy stop order to protect your short position.

- **Sell Stop Order**

  A sell stop order is an order to sell at a price that is lower than the current market price. A sell stop order is mostly used to protect your long positions. Every time you buy a stock or enter a long position, you should place a sell stop order (stop loss) to limit your losses should the market not go in your favour. To illustrate this, let's say I buy 100 shares of Marks & Spencer's at 230p because based on my study, I'm convinced that the share price will rise to around 270p, the next level of resistance. I would also want to protect myself just in case the unexpected happens and the share price drops. I can set a sell stop order at 215p, if the share price drops to 215p, my broker will sell and close my position. If the share price continues to rise, my position remains open and I can take my profit when to price gets to 270p

  You can also use a sell stop order to enter a short position (sell short) at a price that is lower than the current market price. Let's assume Barclays plc is currently trading at 210p. Looking at the charts I am convinced that the share price is about to drop, rather than go ahead and place my order at the market price, I might decide that I want the market to confirm my analysis. I would place a sell stop order to sell Barclays short at 205p. If the share price falls, my order will be executed. If the share price does not fall, my order would not be executed and I would have saved myself from a losing trade.

- **Buy Limit Order**

  A buy limit order is an order to buy a share at a price that is lower than the current market price. A buy limit order is usually used to place a stop to cover short positions.

  It is not advisable to use a buy limit order to buy shares at a price that is lower than the current market price. Most people make the mistake of thinking that if they buy lower than the market price they are getting a bargain. Buying a stock when the price is heading down is like trying to catch a falling knife. In most cases you would get hurt.

- **Sell Limit Order**
  A sell limit order is an order to sell a share at a price that is higher than the current market price. It is usually used to place an order to close and take profits on a long position. Using my Marks & Spencer's example, if I want to take profits at 270p, at the time I buy the shares, I would also place a sell limit order to sell the shares when the price gets to 270p

Determining when to exit a position

Your exit from a position is as important as your entry. Just as you need to have a strategy for your entry, you also need to have a strategy for your exit. You need to think about two different scenarios. The first scenario being how you would exit with a profit and the second scenario, how you would exit with a loss. Nobody likes to make a loss on their investments, but the truth is that you won't make a profit on every trade you place. There are times when the position would not go your way and considering the fact that you do not necessarily want to hold onto a stock "till death do you part", you need to consider the point at which you would accept that you are wrong and exit that position. To ensure that you exit a position with a minimal loss you need to set a stop loss order on the position.

On a similar note, if you are already making a profit on your position you would not want your profit to turn into a loss so you need to have a strategy on how to exit with a profit.

How to determine your stop loss

You should not pick a value "out of the sky" for your stop loss, for instance you should not just decide that the maximum you want to lose on a trade is £100. Since you used the chart to determine your entry, you should also use it to determine your exit. We are going to look at a few strategies that you can use to determine how to set your stop loss.

Using the Average True Range to determine your stop loss

Many traders use the Average True Range (ATR) for setting their stop losses. ATR is a measure of volatility and market noise and it shows a stock's volatility over a given period.

The average true range is the average of the true range for a given period. The true range is the greatest of the following:

- The difference between the current high and the current low
- The difference between the current high and the previous close
- The difference between the current low and the previous close

The average true range is calculated by taking an average of the true ranges over a set number of previous periods. The most popular period used for the average true range is 14. Just like the other indicators we have looked at, don't dwell on the technical details of how to compute the ATR.

The value returned by the average true range is simply an indication as to how a stock is likely to move in any direction during the day (or period on your chart). High values indicate that prices move a lot during the period. Low values indicate that prices do not move that much during the period.

How can you use the average true range in calculating your stop loss? All you do is you subtract a multiple of the average true range from the entry price. The most common value is 2. Using 2, you would take two times the average true range and subtract it from your entry price. For example, if you want to buy a £5 stock whose average true range value was 20 pence, you would simply take a multiple of the average true range (i.e. 20p), and we'd subtract it from your entry price. So, two times your average true range is 40 pence, subtracted from your entry price gives you a stop loss value of £4.60.

Figure 12.1 is a daily chart of Marks and Spencer's and it contains the ATR. The current ATR for Marks and Spencer's as shown on the chart is 9.48p. So let's assume that you want to place an order to buy Marks and Spencer's at 314p and you want to set your stop loss using 2 times the ATR, your stop loss would be set at 314 – (9.48*2) =295.04p

MARKS & SP. ORD 25P (MKS)   26-Jun-2009 Friday
Prev Close:303.00 **O:** 304.25 **H:** 313.25 **L:** 305.25 **C:** 312.00 **V:** 20;51540 **Chg:** 9.00(+2.97 %)

© 2009 MoneyAM.com   www.MoneyAM.ccm

Figure 12.1

Using recent lows or recent highs to determine your stop loss

You can also use recent lows to determine your stop loss. You can decide to exit on a 2 day low, a one week low, a one month low etc. For instance if you decide to exit on a 2 day low, you would need to determine the lowest price that stock has traded with the last 2 days and use that value as your stop loss. Similarly, if you want to exit on a 2 week low, you would need to look at the price pattern of the stock over the last 2 weeks and identify the lowest price that the stock has traded over the last 2 weeks, and then use that price as your stop loss.

Using support and resistance to determine your stop loss

You can also use the most recent support or resistance to determine your stop loss. If you buy a stock (or you open a long position) you can set your stop loss to be slightly below the recent or current support. You can decide to exit the position this way based on the principle that if a stock breaks support, it is likely to continue going lower. However you have to be careful not to place your stop loss to close to the support level because a stock can fall to support and then reverse and continue going higher.

How to exit a position with a profit

The ultimate goal of trading or investing in the stock market is to make a profit. Apart from deciding how to get out if the trade does not go your way, you also need to determine how you are going to exit the trade with a profit. You can do this in 2 ways. First you can set a profit target when you enter a trade. For example let say you buy Tesco shares at 350p, you can set a profit target of 60 pence. This means that you would close your position when the share price of Tesco reaches 410p

Second, you can manage a winning position by monitoring the stock and closing your position if certain conditions occur. For example, you might decide to close a long position if the MACD indicator gives a bearish signal or if RSI drops below 50. Another technique that you can use is to close a long position if the price of the stock falls below a 2 week low.

Chapter 13

Short Selling – Making money when share prices are falling

"Remember, I am neither a bear nor a bull, I am an agnostic opportunist. I want to make money short- and long-term. I want to find good situations and exploit them."

- Jim Cramer

Short selling or **selling short** is the practice of selling a share that the seller does not own. A trader or investor would sell (short) a share with intent of buying it back at a lower price. A short seller attempts to profit from a decline in the price of a share. In short, it is a technique used to make money when share prices are falling.

The short-seller will "borrow" the shares to be sold, and later repurchase shares of the same company for return to the lender. If the share price falls, the short-seller profits from having sold the borrowed shares for more than he later pays to buy them back. However, if the price of the share rises, the short seller loses by having to pay more than the price at which he sold them. The practice is risky in that prices may rise indefinitely, even beyond the net worth of the short seller. The act of repurchasing is known as "buy to cover" or "buy to close".

Short selling is the opposite of buying (also referred to as "going long"). The short seller has a bearish outlook on the share, and to profit from the outlook, intends to "sell high" and "buy low". Traders often use short selling to allow them to profit on trading in stocks which they believe are overvalued and are due for a correction (fall). This is similar to the traditional motive for buying shares, which is to profit on stocks which are undervalued by buying them in anticipation that share price would rise.

For example, assume that shares in Joe Six Pack plc currently sell for £8 per share and the charts are beginning to show bearish signals or bearish sentiment towards the stock. An investor that wants to make a profit from the potential fall in price can borrow 100 shares of Joe Six Pack plc from his broker, thereby allowing him to immediately sell those shares for a total of £800. If the price of Joe Six Pack plc shares later falls to £5 per share, the investor would then buy 100 shares back for £500, then return the shares to the broker and in the process make a profit of £300 (less fees and commissions).

Short selling can be very risky and a trader can incur a loss if the risk is not properly managed. For example, if the shares of Joe Six Pack plc rose to £16, the short seller would have to buy back all the shares at £1600, losing £800. Selling short requires a lot of skill and diligence. The amount you can potentially lose is unlimited in that share prices have no upper limit and can continue to rise indefinitely. For example, while a stock that cost £2 cannot fall below 0p (shares cannot have a negative value), it can rise above £200 and continue rising. It might not happen overnight but it is possible. As an investor you need to remember that the stock market has an upside bias, i.e. in the long run, the stock market rises. Short positions should be considered as short term investments rather than long term.

As mentioned earlier, short selling is the opposite of buying shares when they are going up. To open the trade, the investor "sells short" as opposed to "buying". To close the trade, the investor "buys to cover" as opposed to "selling". Please note that not all stocks are shortable (borrowable). Your broker can advise you on whether or not you can short a particular stock.

Signals to look out for when looking for stocks to sell short

The following are some of the signals to look for on technical indicators when looking to sell a stock short;

- MACD bearish signals
  - When the MACD indicator drops below midline, it is a sign that there is a probability that the price of the underlying stock is about to fall.
  - If the 12 period ma (the faster moving average) crosses the 26 period ma (the faster moving average) from above this is

also a sign that there is a probability that the price of the underlying stock is about to fall.

- RSI bearish signals
    - If RSI falls below midline it is a sign that prices will drop for a while.
    - If RSI drops below 70 from above, it is also a sign the there might be a downward reversal in price of the stock.
- Stochastics bearish signals
    - A bearish crossover from above 80.
- Bearish candlestick signals, i.e. spinning top, bearish engulfing patterns and dark cloud cover patterns
- A bearish 50 day and 200 day moving average crossover, i.e. "death cross".

The most profitable trades would be the ones that are initiated based on simultaneous signals from more than one indicator.

Let's use figure 13.1 to describe a short sell. In March the combined indicators gave a sell signal. Let's assume that as an investor I do not own British Airways shares but I want to take advantage of the predicted fall in share price. To do this, I would sell British Airways shares short (or sell to open) at 240p. I would hold onto this position until I get a corresponding buy signal. In this case, looking at the chart the buy signals were produced at the end of October. To close the position and take a profit I will buy to close (also referred to as buy to cover). In this example, I would buy to cover at around 140p.

In this example my profit will be 100p multiplied by the number of shares sold short, minus any commissions incurred.

Figure 13.1

Figure 13.2 is a weekly chart of Big Lots Inc. The chart contains a few examples of what could have been profitable short selling opportunities. In October 2007 the MACD dropped below midline. This was supported by RSI dropping below 50 and the stochastic indicator also giving a bearish signal.

Study figure 13.3 and try and identify points at which you could have sold short to make a profit. Write your thoughts down on paper. What action would you take (if any) if you were presented with this chart on the 6th of November 2008?

In today's stock market environment you have to understand how to go short, in addition to the traditional method.

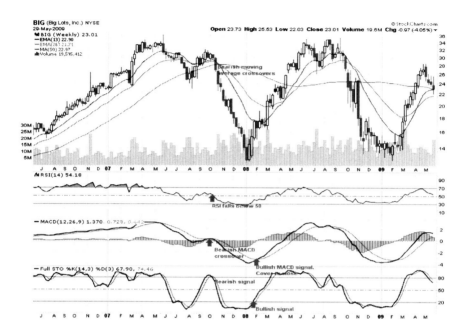

Figure 13.2

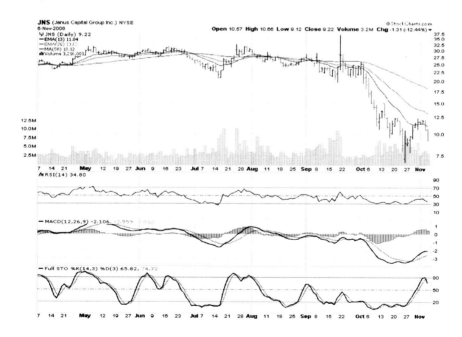

Figure 13.3

Chapter 14

Trading Psychology

"What beat me was not having brains enough to stick to my own game – that is, to play the market only when I was satisfied that precedents favoured my play. There is the plain fool, who does the wrong thing at all times everywhere, but there is also the Wall Street fool, who thinks he must trade all the time. No man can have adequate reasons for buying or selling stocks daily – or sufficient knowledge to make his play an intelligent play."

– Jesse Livermore

Dr Van K Tharp (author of "Trade your way to Financial Freedom") says, *"People make money in the markets by finding themselves, achieving their potential, and getting in tune with the market"*. Being successful in trading is more psychological and behavioural than it is technical.

In this chapter we are going to take a look at some psychological and behavioural aspects of trading. We would look at;

- Fear and greed, and how these two elements of human nature can affect an investor's performance.
- Gambling and speculation and why there is a thin line between the two.
- Discipline and why success cannot be achieved without discipline.
- A trading plan and why not having a trading plan is synonymous to planning to fail.
- A trading journal and why it is important to keep a record of your trades, investments and thoughts.
- Risk and money management and why your long term survival would depend on your ability to properly manage your risk and money.
- Overtrading and how to avoid it.
- The dangers of investment tips, especially unsolicited tips.
- The reasons why most private traders and investors fail.

- Some myths about stocks and investing.

Man's greatest enemies - Fear and Greed

FEAR – False Evidence Appearing Real

"Most often, traders have four fears. There's the fear of being wrong, the fear of losing money, the fear of missing out and the fear of leaving money on the table. I found that basically, those four fears accounted for probably 90% to 95% of the trading errors that we make. Let's put it this way: If you can recognize opportunity, what's going to prevent you from executing your trades properly? Your fear. Your fears immobilize you. Your fears distort your perception of market information in ways that don't allow you to utilize what you know".

- Mark Douglas

Yes, Fear is False Evidence Appearing Real. It's enough to make someone sick. Fear has killed more dreams and ruined more lives than all other causes combined. Fear is man's worst enemy and when it comes to managing or making money, fear causes people to make irrational decisions and in some cases, prevents people from taking appropriate action. The Bible has 365 references of "Fear not" (or "do not be afraid"). That is an equivalent of one per day. One of the most popular quotes from the Old Testament in the Bible is *"That which I feared most has come upon me"*. This was what Job said after he had lost all. In the parable of the talents, also in the Bible, while the stewards that were given five and two talents invested what they were given and were able to double their talents into ten and four respectively, the steward that was given one talent went and hid the talent he was given. He feared that if he invested the talent, he would lose everything. What was the consequence of his action? His talent was taken away from him and given to the steward with 10 talents.

To be a successful stock market investor or speculator you have to learn to manage fear. It's important to say that a small element of fear is necessary because caution is needed in the stock market. For instance, investing your life savings on one particular stock because you think the share price will rise is not absence of fear. It is greed which could have been eliminated with an element of fear. Most investment mistakes are caused by fear or greed.

One way to bring your fear under control is continuous study. According to Ralph Waldo Emerson, *"Knowledge is the antidote to fear"*. The more confident you are about your knowledge, the more confident you'll be to make investment decisions.

Greed

"All human suffering springs from unbridled desire. Unless one extricates oneself from the clutch of greed, one will not free himself from the fetters of sorrow." – Vellopillai Pirapakaran

In the investment world, greed is the cousin of fear. It is equally as fatal as fear. It is greed that makes people think they can make millions from the stock market without much effort. It is greed that makes people subscribe to courses that promise overnight success and millions in the stock market. It is greed that makes people buy shares on tips, thinking that they can make a 100% or more within days. Internet marketers and "pump and dump" stock market tipsters recognise and take advantage of the fact that human beings are controlled by greed. It is greed that causes people to lose their life savings in the stock market.

As I mentioned earlier, most investment mistakes are caused by fear or greed, and until an investor learns to free himself from the bondage of greed, he would not be able to free himself from the pain of losses.

Gambling versus Speculation

In his biography, Reminiscences of a Stock Operator, Jesse Livermore, a legendary stock speculator said of his early days as a speculator *"Yet, I can see now that my main trouble was my failure to grasp the vital difference between stock gambling and stock speculation".*

Another relevant quote from his book is *"Since suckers always lose money when they gamble in stocks – they never really speculate"*.

As a trader or an investor it is very important to understand that there is a very thin line between gambling and speculation. You want to be speculator not a gambler. Gambling is defined in the dictionary as; *to play at any game of chance for money or other stakes; to stake or risk money, or anything of value, on the outcome of something involving chance; a venture in a game of chance for stakes, especially for high stakes.* Speculation on the other hand is defined as; *engagement in business transactions involving considerable risk but offering the chance of large gains, especially trading in commodities, stocks, etc., in the hope of profit from changes in the market price; a conclusion or opinion reached by such contemplation.* From the above definitions you can see that both words have similar meaning. Both involve predicting the outcome of an event. However, if we shift away from the definitions in the dictionary, while gambling is synonymous to taking an uneducated guess, speculation is synonymous to taking an educated and calculated guess. While the odds are against a gambler, the odds are in favour of the speculator. According to Dickson G Watts in his book Speculation as a Fine Art, *"Speculation is a venture based upon calculation. Gambling is a venture without calculation".* The law makes this distinction, it sustains speculation and condemns gambling.

How do you avoid being a stock gambler? First and foremost, you must always trade with a plan. Plan your trade and trade your plan. If you trade without a plan, then you have engaged in gambling not speculation. For example, if I leave home in the morning without any intention of buying or selling a share, but during lunch I notice that a stock, say Sainsbury's has risen 5% on the day. If I then decide to buy 100 shares of Sainsbury anticipating that it will rise further, my action will be classified as a gamble rather than speculation. Such acts if done consistently would lead to loses in the long run.

Also, if I continually violate my methods, for instance buying when the slope of the moving averaging is falling, or if I repeat the same mistakes time and time again, then I am tending towards gambling rathor than spoculation.

My desire is that after reading this book you would not engage in gambling.

Discipline

To be successful in the stock market you need to be disciplined. If you are a private investor you need a lot of self-discipline as you are not directly accountable to anyone for your actions. Elbert Hubbard defined self-discipline as, "*the ability to make yourself do what you should do, when you should do it, whether you feel like it or not.*" As a trader you should do what is right and not try to take shortcuts. There are no shortcuts to success.

Here are some things you can do towards becoming more self-disciplined.

- **Determine the amount of time you want to devote to trading and stick to it.**

    It is essential that from the start that you decide on the amount of time that you want to devote to trading. It could be 1 hour a day, 2 hours a day, or even 1 hour a week. You must also try your best to stick to the allocated time. Trading can be very addictive and you must not allow it to take over your live.

- **Always follow your plan.**

    There's a popular saying, "failing to plan is planning to fail". You need to have a trading plan and you need to stick to your plan. Having a trading plan helps to eliminate impulse buying/trading. A plan will also serve as a guide to exit if your trade is not going according to plan.

- **Keep a trading journal.**

    You have to keep a record of all your trades. Your records should state your reasons for buying or selling, your thoughts at that point in time, your reasons for closing your position and whether you were right or wrong.

- **Always use stop losses.**
  You should always protect your trades with a stop loss. This is absolutely necessary if you are trading part time and you do not monitor the market all day long. It also helps to reduce your stress levels as you know ahead how much you are likely to loss if the trade does not go in your favour.

- **Get rid of bad habits.**
  Nothing is more powerful than habit. We are slaves to our own habits. To succeed in trading you need to deal with bad habits such as impulsive trading, indecision, lack of organisation, etc.

Developing Your Trading Plan

"Write the vision, and make it plain on tablets that he may run who reads it"

The Bible, Habakkuk 2 v 2

As the saying goes, failing to plan is planning to fail, it is absolutely necessary that you have a trading plan. Your trading plan is like a roadmap. It reminds you about what you set out to achieve and how you intend to achieve it. Trading without a plan is like setting out on a journey without knowing your destination and how to get there. Your plan should include the following;

- **What markets/shares are you covering?**
  It is absolutely essential that you do not try to cover too many markets, sectors or shares. As time goes on you would find out that you can make a lot more money by focusing on a small number of companies or markets than trying to follow everything on the market. According to Warren Buffet "If you have a harem of 40 women, you never get to know any of them very well".

- **What timeframe are you focusing on?**
  Your trading plan should include what timeframes you are focusing on. If you are trading part time, you should focus on swing trading or position trading rather than day trading. You

should also be studying daily charts and weekly charts rather than intraday charts.

- **What will trigger your entries and exits?**

  Your trading plan should also state what would trigger your entries and exits, e.g. moving average crossover, new high, RSI moving above 50, etc.

- **Are you disciplined enough to implement your plan once it is developed?**

  This is a question that you have to ask yourself. If the answer is no, then you have to work on your self-disciple. You have to have a military style discipline if you want to make money from trading.

Keeping a Trading Journal

Keeping a trading journal is a very important aspect of your trading. Your journal should state your reasons for buying or selling, your thoughts at that point in time, your reasons for closing your position and whether you were right or wrong.

You should also keep a journal of your thoughts about the markets and stocks that you review. You can revisit your journal to see if your assumptions turned out to be right or wrong.

Risk and Money Management

"Experienced traders control risk, inexperienced traders chase gains."

-Alan Farley

Proper risk and money management is essential for your long term success. You should only risk a certain amount of your capital (account) on any trade. The amount you can risk will determine whether or not you should be taking the trade. Opinions as to how much you should risk on a trade vary depending on who you speak to. Some professional say 2%, some 5%, and some 10%. In my opinion, the amount you can risk will depend on your capital and your risk appetite, although it should never exceed 10%. Below is an example of how you can determine how much to invest in any one trade;

Capital Base	Maximum Risk (%)
>10,000	2% of your capital
1,000 – 9,999	5% of your capital
<1,000	10% of your capital

Based on the above, if your capital is £800, you should not risk (or lose) more than £80 on any one trade. Assuming you are buying shares the traditional way, you need to consider the cost of commissions. Let's assume your broker charges £12.50 as commission, to complete the trade (i.e. open and close) you would pay around £25 in commission charges. That means using our example of an £800 account, you can risk £55 on the trade. This means if the trade goes against you, you should not lose more than £55. Taking this into consideration, if you buy 100 shares of a particular company, say Tesco, you have to exit the trade if the value of the share price falls by more than 55p (55p * 100 = £55) from your entry level. Let's say you bought the shares at 400p per share, you have to close the trade if it falls to 345p per share.

Having said that, your stop loss should be determined by other factors as described in previous chapters. However, if your ideal stop loss (based on the factors you have taken into consideration) is greater than the maximum amount you should risk, then you should not take that trade. For example using the £800 capital, if your stop loss is calculated to be 110p away from your entry, then you either buy 50 shares (110p * 50 = £55) or you should skip that trade and look for one that is more suitable to your capital.

You might have heard about people that lost all their capital on one or two trades. This is practically impossible if you adhere to risk management principles. Using the £800 to illustrate, if your maximum risk for each trade is 10%, you should still have almost £280 capital left if you have 10 consecutive losing trades. However, this should not happen, because if you have 3 consecutive losing trades, you should go back to the drawing board and review your trading plan. Remember, your trading should be treated as a business, not a pastime.

Overtrading

In business, a business is said to be overtrading when it tries to engage in more business than the investment in working capital will allow. In most cases overtrading is a by-product of greed and fear and it can lead to an investor's ruin.

Overtrading comes in various forms. Three of the most common instances are;

1) When an investor enters a position that is too excessive for his account, i.e. he is risking more than the maximum allowed by his risk management criteria.
2) When an investor opens and closes too many positions within a given period, relative to the size of his account. For example, if the account size (capital) is £1000 and an investor opens and closes about 5 positions a week, then he is overtrading.

3) When an investor has too many positions open at the same time. It's very difficult to manage too many open positions. When you have a number of potential trades, instead of taking every position and hope that you would break even, it is better to further analyse the trades and see which ones give you the best reward to risk ratio.

An investor has to be disciplined to resist overtrading.

Investment Tips

It would be incomplete to talk about investment psychology without mentioning tips. Tips have been around since the stock market has been in existence. An entire chapter was devoted to tips in Jesse Livermore's biography, the Reminiscences of a Stock Market Operator.

Jesse Livermore noted that people want tips. He noted that people crave not only to get tips but also to give them. Even intelligent people seek for tips. People's appetite for tips is what fuels the existence of stock market scams. Pump and dump schemes are an example of stock market scams. The Internet has made this type of scam very popular as it offers a cheap and easy way of reaching a large numbers of potential investors. The schemes involves a stock promoter, usually a marketer that is promoting himself as a stock market expert, sending an email or newsletter that promotes a company as the goldmine whose share price is about to explode (increase exponentially). They might pretend to be giving some insider information, for example, they might say the company has just won a contract worth millions of dollars or they might say the company has just made a major discovery of natural resources. The promoters lure investors into buying these penny shares only for investors to find out that instead of rising, the price of the stock falls dramatically.

Pump and Dump Schemes

Here's an extract from the U.S Securities and Exchange Commission regarding pump and dump schemes;

"Pump and dump" schemes, also known as "hype and dump manipulation," involve the touting of a company's stock (typically microcap companies) through false and misleading statements to the marketplace. After pumping the stock, fraudsters make huge profits by selling their cheap stock into the market.

Pump and dump schemes often occur on the Internet where it is common to see messages posted that urge readers to buy a stock quickly or to sell before the price goes down, or a telemarketer will call using the same sort of pitch. Often the promoters will claim to have "inside" information about an impending development or to use an "infallible" combination of economic and stock market data to pick stocks. In reality, they may be company insiders or paid promoters who stand to gain by selling their shares after the stock price is "pumped" up by the buying frenzy they create. Once these fraudsters "dump" their shares and stop hyping the stock, the price typically falls, and investors lose their money.

You can also check this website for more information about pump and dump schemes. http://www.sec.gov/investor/pubs/pump.htm

The following image is an example of what a pump and dump scam might look like;

Boiler Room Scams

Another example of a stock market scam is the boiler room scam. This is similar to the pump and bump scam but in this case the promoter uses cold calling rather than the Internet. The promoters have a way of getting hold of phone numbers of potential investors.

They call investors, introduce themselves as working for a major hedge fund or investment house, and try to sell shares of a company convincing the investor that these shares are about to double in price. If they are able to convince an investor to buy, they then ask the investor to pay funds into an account. In most cases the investor either ends up with shares that are worthless or can loss their money altogether.

Here's an extract from the UK's Financial Services Authority's (FSA) website regarding share scams;

Share scams

(also known as boiler room scams)

REMEMBER: IF IT SOUNDS TOO GOOD TO BE TRUE, IT PROBABLY IS!

It sounds obvious, but if a stranger rings you out of the blue and tries to sell you shares in companies you've probably never even heard of - take great care. They may be part of a financial scam using hard-sell tactics to persuade you to buy shares.

If you buy them, you may be left with potentially worthless shares. You may also have no rights to complain or claim compensation from the relevant UK schemes as most of these boiler room scams are based overseas.

The first time you hear from such firms could be by post or email, or they might advertise their services over the internet. They may offer you a free research report into a company in which you hold shares, or a free gift or a discount on their dealing charges. "Nothing to lose", you think, "and it's free". So you sign on the dotted line and send your response in the freepost envelope. You think it must be OK because it's got a UK address, so if anything goes wrong, you'll be able to complain.

BUT:

- By signing on the dotted line, you have probably agreed to be contacted by the firm in the future. This was probably written in the small print of the mailshot.
- The UK freepost address on the return envelope may simply be a forwarding address to an overseas address.

If you have been contacted by an unauthorised overseas firm in this way, please help the FSA by giving us information on your dealings with them.

Other share scams

If you already own shares in a company, including those traded on AIM, you may receive a call from someone offering to buy your shares, usually at a higher price than their market value.

If the price of your shares is low, the offer will probably sound very attractive to you. They will also ask you to pay something up front, as a **bond** or other form of **security**, which they say you'll get back if the sale doesn't go ahead. They could also ask you to sign a form preventing you from disclosing details of the offer.

Don't be fooled by such an approach! It's probably no more than an advance fee scam – where you give them your money and never hear back from them again. They can be very persistent, phoning you many times and even sending you documents or forms to complete.

Reasons why many private traders and investors fail

According to research more than 90% of traders lose money. The accuracy of this has not been established, however, it's a fact that more traders lose than win. Here are a few reasons why traders lose.

- **Not understanding the mechanics behind fluctuations in share prices**

Most people fail to understand that in a bull market, or an uptrend, share prices do not rise every day. Similarly in a bear market, or a downtrend, share prices do not fall every day. Not fully understanding this concepts make people panic and sell a profitable position during a bull market. It also pushes people to buy shares during a bear market. Successful traders and investors understand that a temporary fall in price during a bull market might be a pullback, not necessarily a reversal. They understand that they have to be able to sit tight until there indicators give a reversal signal.

- **Trying to keep track of too many markets.**
  Most private traders try to keep track of too many markets, e.g., stocks, commodities, Forex etc. The danger of doing this is that the person is unable to focus. Even professionals working for top investment banks or hedge funds tend to focus on a few sectors or industries. For example, an analyst that covers the Energy sector is unlikely to cover the Telecoms sector. You need to select a few sectors and a set number of stocks and track your selection on a regular basis. If one of the stocks in your selection is forming a pattern and looks like it might be a potential trade, then add that stock to your watch list and track it regularly. If you don't do this, you would find out that you are missing so many trades that could have been profitable.

- **Inability to keep emotions separate from trading.**
  Trading and emotions don't mix. Greed, fear and pride would lead to substantial loses.

- **Unmanaged Expectations**
  Most people start trading because they have been told that it is the easiest route to becoming a millionaire, or because they have been told that on completion of a one day course, they can start making £500 a day without much effort. Even though £500 per day is achievable, it is not what you would make as a beginner. It would take time and going through a process to achieve this figure, especially if you are a private trader and you only trade part time. Apart from that, most courses and advertisements don't tell people how much capital they would need to be able to make £500 per day. Using a reward to risk ratio of 3:1, you

would have to risk around £170 to make a £500 profit. If you use my recommendations on the maximum risk per trade, then you would need to have an account size of at least £3,400 to be able to take the trade.

- **Trading without a plan**

  Most private traders trade without a trading plan. This means that they are gambling and just hoping that things work out in their favour. This is the wrong way to go about trading. According to Victor Hugo, *"He who every morning plans the transactions of the day and follows that plan, carries a thread that will guide him through the labyrinth of the most busy life."* Having a properly documented plan for every trade would reduce the number of unplanned trades and increase your potential to succeed.

- **Not identifying and addressing individual weaknesses**

  Another reason most traders fail is not a lack of methodology, but because they fail to address certain habits or psychological issues that are detrimental to trading. According to Jesse Livermore, *"A trader, in addition to studying basic conditions, remembering market precedents and keeping in mind the psychology of the outside public as well as the limitations of his brokers, must also know himself and provide against his own weaknesses."* As human beings, we find it difficult to admit our weaknesses and this is one characteristic that we take into trading. Unfortunately, to succeed as a trader you have to be able to analyse your behaviour and response to the various situations that you are presented. You have to identify your weaknesses and protect yourself from them. There is a saying that goes "we have known the enemy and the enemy is us". In trading, you are your own enemy, not your broker, not the market, not the external forces. According to Rob Gilbert *"First we form habits, then they form us. Conquer your bad habits or they will conquer you"*.

Four Myths about Stocks and Investing

Here are four myths about trading and stock market investing;

- **The stock cannot fall any further.**
  Most people assume that if a company's share price has fallen by a certain amount, it is highly impossible to fall any further. Share prices fall as a result of various factors. It could be that the company has reduced its growth estimate, or just that the company has fallen out of favour with analysts. The stock market is to a very large extent speculation. A falling share price could mean that there is speculation that the company might be about to experience difficult times. If a company's share price has fallen 50%, it can still fall by a further 50%. It's even possible for shares of historically good companies to become worthless. In the UK, Northern Rock is a very good example. In the US, Lehman Brothers is a very good example.

- **The stock cannot rise any further.**
  Similarly a lot of people assume that because a company's share price has tripled in value, it is very unlikely for it to rise any further. A share price can rise to a level that defies explanation. This is seen in a lot of technological and biotech stocks.

- **You have to be smart to succeed.**
  This is also untrue. Trading is not an activity where the person with the biggest intellect wins. *"The most important quality for an investor is temperament, not intellect... You need a temperament that neither derives great pleasure from being with the crowd or against the crowd."* Results in investing is best summarised by this quote by Adeola Odutola a Nigerian industrialist, *"Over the years I have known too many people who are not terribly intelligent but who somehow get things done slowly and perhaps not imaginatively, but they get there. Yet too many able people who understand much better and see much more clearly and talk much clearly get nothing done. Hence, I have observed that effectiveness is neither a talent nor ability. It is a practice, a habit"*

- **Trading is for the fast and furious.**
  Even though certain timeframes, e.g. day trading requires speed and the ability to make quick decisions, trading as a whole requires a lot of patience. According to Warren Buffet, *"The Stock Market is designed to transfer money from the Active to the Patient"*. Seth Glickenhaus puts it in this context, *"You make money on Wall Street by being very selective and being patient, waiting for those opportunities that are irresistible, where the percentages are very heavily in your favor"*.

Review your Performance Regularly

As a private trader or investor, you would have to conduct a regular performance review of your trading. You would need to analysis your total number of trades, the number of plan and unplanned trades. You would also need to analyse your win/loss ratio and total profit or loss for the period. As you haven't got a manager, you would have to manage yourself. If you are underperforming or making a loss you would need to put yourself on a performance improvement plan.

Take a break once in a while

There are times when you would need to take a break from the markets. Two instances when you might want to take a break are;

1. **When the market lacks direction, i.e. up one day, down the next.**
   The Bible has the phrase *"To everything there is a season"*. In the stock market there is a time to buy, there is a time to sell and there is a time to refrain from buying and selling. It is very difficult to be a profitable investor when the market lacks direction. During such periods it's best to stay on the sidelines, preserve capital and resume activity once the market starts to move in one direction.

2. When you are not performing well

If you are not performing well, i.e. your average losses are greater than your average gains you should stop trading with real money for a while. If this happens take a break, then try your strategies out on a virtual platform and only return to using real money if you are making a profit on the virtual platform.

Chapter 15

Wisdom for Investing

Wisdom is the principle thing; Therefore get wisdom. And in all your getting, get understanding. - The Bible, Proverbs 4 v 7

This chapter is one of the most important chapters in this book. You'll win or lose depending on the amount of wisdom you acquire and apply. In this chapter I'm going to present some quotes relating to trading and add some commentary to them. Some of the quotes might appear elsewhere in this book don't see this as a repetition, it is more of an emphasis on the importance of the message within the quote. Consider the quotes as nuggets of wisdom and food for thought. Don't just browse through them, meditate on them and think about how they can be relevant to your success as an investor.

Quotes on Patience

"We don't get paid for activity, just for being right. As to how long we'll wait, we'll wait indefinitely." – Warren Buffet

"The Stock Market is designed to transfer money from the Active to the Patient." – Warren Buffet

"You do things when the opportunities come along. I've had periods in my life when I've had a bundle of ideas come along, and I've had long dry spells. If I get an idea next week, I'll do something. If not, I won't do a damn thing." – Warren Buffet

"You make money on wall street by being very selective and being patient, waiting for those opportunities that are irresistible, where the percentages are very heavily in your favor."- Seth Glickenhaus

"The secret of long-term investment success is benign neglect. Don't try too hard. Much success can be attributed in inactivity." – Warren Buffet

114

My Comments

Investing in the stock market is not a game in which the fastest guy wins. In fact, the proverb "the patient dog eats the fattest bone" is very true when it comes to the stock market. You have to remember the reason why you are investing. You are investing to make money, so it's best to wait for strong signals that have a very high probability of profit rather than take anything that comes your way.

Quotes on Strategy

"Profits can be made safely only when the opportunity is available and not just because they happen to be desired or needed. ...Willingness and ability to hold funds uninvested while awaiting real opportunities is a key to success in the battle for investment survival."- Gerald Loeb

"What beat me was not having brains enough to stick to my own game – that is, to play the market only when I was satisfied that precedents favoured my play. There is the plain fool, who does the wrong thing at all times everywhere, but there is also the Wall Street fool, who thinks he must trade all the time. No man can have adequate reasons for buying or selling stocks daily – or sufficient knowledge to make his play an intelligent play."– Jesse Livermore

"Don't move unless it is advantageous, Do not execute unless it is effective, Do not challenge unless it is critical" - Sun Tzu in The Art of War

"You win or lose, live or die – and the difference is just an eyelash" - Douglas MacArthur, General

My Comments

Just like most things in life you need to have a strategy to win. In chess you need to have a reason and strategy behind every move, the same applies to investing in the stock market. Ask yourself these questions; what is my strategy? What am I trying to achieve?

Quotes on Research

"I never buy anything unless I can fill out on a piece of paper my reasons. I may be wrong, but I would know the answer to that. "I'm paying $32 billion today for the Coca Cola Company because..." If you can't answer that question, you shouldn't buy it. If you can answer that question, and you do it a few times, you'll make a lot of money." – Warren Buffet

"Twenty years in this business convinces me that any normal person using the customary 3% of the brain can pick stocks as well as, if not better, than the average Wall Street expert." – Peter Lynch

"Investing without research is like playing poker without looking at the cards." – Peter Lynch

My Comments

You have to do your research before committing a penny to any stock. Have you identified the trend? Have you identified support and resistance points? Have you studied the stock reacted to your chosen indicators performed in the past?

Quotes on Risk Management

"It's only when the tide goes out that you learn who's been swimming naked." – Warren Buffet

"It takes 20 years to build a reputation and five minutes to ruin it. If you think about that, you'll do things differently." – Warren Buffet

"I can't sleep" answered the nervous one.
"Why not?" asked the friend.
"I am carrying so much cotton that I can't sleep thinking about. It is wearing me out. What can I do?"
Sell down to the sleeping point", answered the friend.

My Comments

It's important that you never risk more than you can afford to lose, but it's equally important to make sure that you do not get wiped out in a single trade. Make sure that the amount you have invested in a stock does not 'steal' your peace.

Quotes on Emotional Intelligence

"An investor's worst enemy is not the stock market but his own emotions." Benjamin Graham

"Temperament costs investors more than ignorance." – Benjamin Graham

"The most important quality for an investor is temperament, not intellect... You need a temperament that neither derives great pleasure from being with the crowd or against the crowd." – Warren Buffett

"Success in investing doesn't correlate with I.Q. once you're above the level of 25. Once you have ordinary intelligence, what you need is the temperament to control the urges that get other people into trouble in investing." – Warren Buffett

"Everyone has the brain power to make money in stocks. Not everyone has the stomach." – Peter Lynch

My Comments

When it comes to investing in the stock market your emotions can be your best friend and also your worst enemy. You need to keep your emotions under control. Establish the trend and don't get too excited about the daily or intraday fluctuations.

Quotes on Protecting Yourself

"A trader, in addition to studying basic conditions, remembering market precedents and keeping in mind the psychology of the outside public as well as the limitations of his brokers, must also know himself and provide against his own weaknesses." - Jesse Livermore

"It sounds very easy to say that all you have to do is to watch the tape, establish your resistance points and be ready to trade along the line of least resistance as soon as you have determined it. But in actual practice a man has to guard against many things, and most of all against himself – that is, against human nature." - Jesse Livermore

My Comments

You need to identify your weaknesses and put some safeguards in place to protect you from them. For example, if you are easily moved by intraday fluctuations then don't check share prices during the day.

Quotes on Planning

"Write the vision, and make it plain on tablets that he may run who reads it" - The Bible, Habakkuk 2 v 2

"For which of you, intending to build a tower, does not sit down first and count the cost, whether he has enough to finish it" - The Bible, Luke 14 v 28

"My plan of trading was sound enough and won oftener than lost. If I had stuck to it I'd have been right perhaps as often as seven out of ten times" – Jesse Livermore

My Comments

Your plan is your blueprint. If you do not have a plan, you don't have anything to aim for. Likewise if you don't stick to your plan, you can't expect to get the results you desire.

Quotes on Dedication

"I know the price of success: dedication, hard work, and an unremitting devotion to the things you want to see happen" - Frank Lloyd Wright

"A man can be as great as he wants to be. If you believe in yourself and have the courage, the determination, the dedication, the competitive drive and if you are willing to sacrifice the little things in life and pay the price for the things that are worthwhile, it can be done." – Vince Lombardi

"For an interest to be rewarding, one must pay in discipline and dedication, especially through the difficult or boring stages which are inevitably encountered" - Mira Komarovsky

"The concentration and dedication- the intangibles are the deciding factors between who won and who lost". -Tom Seaver

"Determine what specific goal you want to achieve. Then dedicate yourself to its attainment with unswerving "singleness of purpose, the trenchant zeal of a crusader". -Paul J. Meyer

"Keep your dreams alive. Understand to achieve anything requires faith and belief in yourself, vision, hard work, determination, and dedication. Remember all things are possible for those who believe." – Gail Devers

My Comments

To be a successful investor you have to be dedicated to what you are doing. Dedication here does not mean checking charts every hour or even every day. It means that you are dedicated to building wealth. It means you are dedicated to your plan and you are dedicated to you style. If for instance you embark on a fitness plan which requires that you exercise 3 times a week, you won't get results if you don't stick to your regime. Sticking to your regime requires dedication to the course. It's the same with investing; you have to be dedicated to your original goals.

Quotes on Tips

"The average man doesn't wish to be told that it is a bull or a bear market. What he desires is to be told specifically which particular stock to buy or sell. He wants to get something for nothing. He does not wish to work. He doesn't even wish to have to think." – Jesse Livermore

"I know from experience that nobody can give me a tip or series of tips that will make more money for me than my own judgment" – Jesse Livermore

My Comments

You can't build wealth by depending on tips, you need to develop a system for identifying your own trades. People's appetite for tips is what allows boiler room and pump and dump scams to be popular. In fact your stock charts should be considered your greatest tipster because it provides you with all the information you need.

Quotes on Fear, Greed, Hope, Ignorance and Folly

"The fact that people will be full of greed, fear or folly is predictable. The sequence is not predictable." – Warren Buffet

"The speculator's deadly enemies are: Ignorance, greed, fear and hope. All the statute books in the world and all the rules of all the Exchanges on earth cannot eliminate these from the human animal." – Jesse Livermore

"The speculator's chief enemies are always boring from within. It is inseparable from human nature to hope and to fear. In speculation when the market goes against you, you hope that every day will be the last day - and you lose more than you should had you not listened to hope ... And when the market goes your way you become fearful that the next day will take away your profit, and you get out-too soon. Fear keeps you from making as much money as you ought to. The successful trader has to fight these two deep-seated instincts. He has to reverse what you might call his natural impulses. Instead of hoping he must fear; instead of fearing he must hope. He must fear that his loss may develop into a much bigger loss, and hope that his profit may become a big profit. It is absolutely wrong to gamble in stocks the way the average man does." – Jesse Livermore

Other notable quotes

"When I'm bearish and I sell a stock, each sale must be at a lower level than the previous sale. When I am buying, the reverse is true. I must buy on a rising scale. I don't buy long stocks on a scale down, I buy on a scale up." Jesse Livermore

"The price pattern reminds you that every movement of importance is but a repetition of similar price movements, that just as soon as you can familiarize yourself with the actions of the past, you will be able to

anticipate and act correctly and profitably upon forthcoming movements." – Jesse Livermore

"This market right now is moving on nothing more than emotions. Guess what? It almost always moves on emotions." - David Bach

"The only way you get a real education in the market is to invest cash, track your trade, and study your mistakes!" - Jesse Livermore

"Any time you think you have the game conquered, the game will turn around and punch you right in the nose." - Mike Schmidt

"Even a thief takes ten years to learn his trade. " - Source: (Japanese)

"Be Patient, Be deliberate. Wait for the perfect setup. When you see it don't hesitate. If it's not happening, don't take action" - Entries & Exits

"If a stock doesn't act right don't touch it; because being unable to tell precisely what is wrong, you cannot tell which way it is going. No diagnosis, no prognosis. No prognosis, no profit." – Jesse Livermore

"The professional concerns himself with doing the right thing rather than making money, knowing that profit takes care of itself if the other things are attended to. - Jesse Livermore

"The stock market is a no-called-strike game. You don't have to swing at everything--you can wait for your pitch. The problem when you're a money manager is that your fans keep yelling, 'Swing, you bum!'" – Warren Buffet

"Rule No.1: Never lose money. Rule No.2: Never forget rule No.1." – Warren Buffet

"The elements of good trading are cutting losses, cutting losses and cutting losses." Ed Seykota.

"The only time I really ever lost money was when I broke my own rules." – Jesse Livermore.

Wisdom – The Investor's Life Jacket

Just like a life jacket is designed to keep a person afloat on water, wisdom is what saves the investor from ruin. Let me use the following passage from the Bible (Proverbs chapter 7 verses 1 – 27) to illustrate;

"My son, keep my words,
And treasure my commands within you.
Keep my commands and live,
And my law as the apple of your eye.
Bind them on your fingers;
Write them on the tablet of your heart.
Say to wisdom, "you are my sister,"
And call understanding your nearest kin,
That they may keep you from the immoral woman,
From the seductress who flatters with her words."

It might seem a bit extreme to compare the stock market to a seductress. However, if you think about it, a seductress is simply a woman who seduces and the stock market is the greatest seducer of all. It doesn't matter whether you call yourself an investor, trader, or speculator you have to guard yourself against the seductress. How do you do that? By applying wisdom and getting understanding. The passage from the Bible goes on to tell us what happened to the man that lacked wisdom.

"For at the window of my house
I looked through my lattice,
And saw among the simple,
I perceived among the youths,
A young man devoid of understanding,
Passing along the street near her corner;
And he took the path to her house ......

...... And there a woman met him,
With the attire of a harlot, and a crafty heart.
She was loud and rebellious ....

.......With her enticing speech she caused him to yield,

With her flattering lips she seduced him.
Immediately he went after her, as an ox goes to the slaughter,
Or as a fool to the correction of the stocks,
Till an arrow struck his liver.
As a bird hastens to the snare,
He did not know it would cost him his life."

The passage ends like this;

" .... Do not stray into her paths;
For she has cast down many wounded,
And all who were slain by her were strong men....."

If you've been around long enough you'll find out that the stock market is enticing. So many shares are calling out to you. Volatile shares are the most tempting ones. There are also a lot of fraudulent tipsters out there. They are always sending emails or using other forms of communication to ask investors to part with their money, promising them over 100% returns in a few weeks (an enticing speech). Many investors don't realise that falling for the temptation can cost them their life savings.

To overcome the seductress you need to have a solid background and be equipped with wisdom.

The Road Less Taken

To be a successful investor you have to take the road less travelled. The road tiled with discipline, diligence, determination and patience. The road that looks boring. The following poem illustrates taking the road less taken, i.e. the road that leads to profits.

Two roads diverged in a yellow wood,
And sorry I could not travel both
And be one traveller, long I stood
And looked down one as far as I could

To where it bent in the undergrowth;

Then took the other, as just as fair,
And having perhaps the better claim,
Because it was grassy and wanted wear;
Though as for that the passing there
Had worn them really about the same,

And both that morning equally lay
In leaves no step had trodden black.
Oh, I kept the first for another day!
Yet knowing how way leads on to way,
I doubted if I should ever come back.

I shall be telling this with a sigh
Somewhere ages and ages hence:
Two roads diverged in a wood, and I—
I took the one less travelled by,
And that has made all the difference

-   Robert Frost

Make Wisdom your Code of Conduct

I'll like to implore you to ponder on the quotes that have been mentioned in this chapter and consider how they can improve your trading and investing. Make the quotes and illustrations in this chapter your code of conduct. I'll like to conclude this chapter with another quote from the Bible. In the book of Joshua, God gave this commandment to Joshua, *"This Book of the Law shall not depart from your mouth, but you shall meditate in it day and night that you may observe to do according to all that is written in it. For then you will make your way prosperous, and then you will have good success"*. Select the one's that you like the most and paste them by your trading diary or computer.

Chapter 16

Generating your Charts

"The market does not beat them. They beat themselves, because though they have brains they cannot sit tight."

- Jesse Livermore

If you are not a beginner, I'll like to crave your indulgence at this point as you might find this chapter a bit elementary. In this chapter we are going to create some basic stock charts. We are going to use the charting facilities available on moneyam.com for UK stocks and stockcharts.com for US stocks. This chapter is instructional and to get the best out of it you should ideally be logged onto a computer with Internet access.

Generating charts on MoneyAM.com

Open up your Internet browser and type http://www.moneyam.com in the url field. To be able to use the charting facilities on this website you would have to register and create a user account. Basic registration is free. Make sure you select the free registration option, as that is all you need to use the charting facilities.

When you are logged on to MoneyAM.com, click on the **Charts** option in the menu. You should have a screen similar to the one below.

The chart defaults to a chart showing UKX. UKX is the symbol (also called 'ticker') for the FTSE 100. To personalise the chart perform the following tasks;

- Click on the Size dropdown option and change the size to 900.
- In the EMA section click on the boxes beside 13 and 25.
- In the Indicators section click on the boxes beside MACD, Slow Stoch and RSI.

  You now have a daily line chart of the FTSE 100. Let's change it `to a candle chart.

- Click on the round button beside Candle in the Type section around the top of your screen.

You now have a daily candle chart of the FTSE 100

Now bring out your pen and paper, study the chart carefully and write down your thoughts on the indicators and where you think the index is heading.

After you've written your thoughts let's generate the charts of a few UK stocks.

To generate a chart of Cadbury's PLC, type CBRY (the stock market symbol for Cadbury's) in the box beside Stock Symbol on your MoneyAM screen, and then click on the 'Draw Chart' tab. You should now have a chart of Cadbury's plc. Study the chart carefully and write down your thoughts on the indicators and where you think the stock is heading and what you think might happen over the next few days.

Now repeat the chart generation process for the following stocks;

BARC	Barclays
RBS	Royal Bank of Scotland
BAY	British Airways
PRU	Prudential
IHG	Intercontinental Hotels Group
REX	Rexam
BDEV	Barratt Development
LAM	Lamprell Plc
BP	British Petroleum
BAE	British Aerospace

You can find some more stock symbols on Yahoo! Finance. Type the following link into your browser,

http://uk.finance.yahoo.com/q/cp?s=%5EFTSE

Generating charts on Stockcharts.com

Open up your Internet browser and type

http://www.stockcharts.com in the url. You don't need to register on this website to use their free charting facilities.

When you on the stockcharts.com homepage, type DELL in the box beside Symbol in the 'Create a Chart' section at the top of the screen and click on 'Go'. You should have a chart similar to the one below.

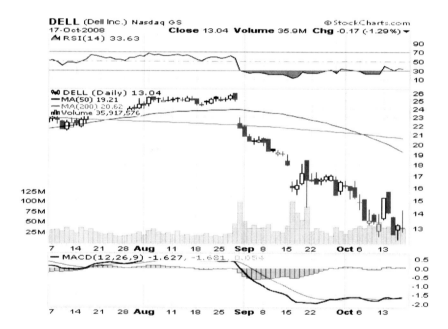

At the bottom of the screen there is a chart control panel like the one below.

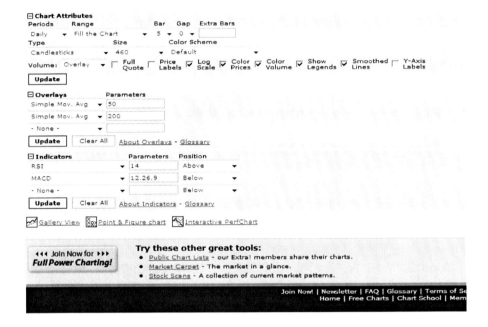

Now change the following options on the charts;

- Change 'Size' to700. To do this, click on the down arrow beside the default size of 460 and then click on 700.

- Change the first Simple Moving Average to 13. To do this, click on the Parameters box beside first 'Simple Mov. Avg' box and type 13.

- Change the second Simple Moving Average to 26. To do this, click on the Parameters box beside second 'Simple Mov. Avg' box and type 26.

In the Indicators section;

- Change the RSI position to 'below'

- Add Full Stochastics by clicking on the arrow beside 'None', and selecting 'Full Stochastics'. Leave the default options.

Click on **Update** to update the chart. Your chart should look like the chart below.

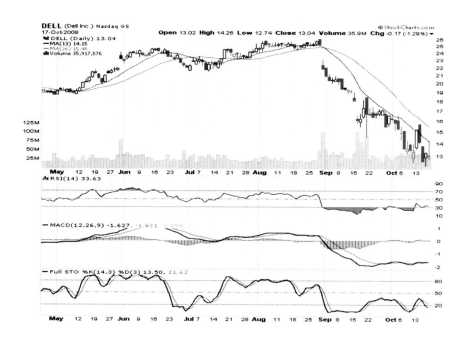

Now generate the charts for the following stocks, typing the stock symbol and clicking update.

INTC	Intel
YHOO	Yahoo
EBAY	EBay
AA	Alcoa
C	Citigroup
AMD	Advanced Micro Devices
CSCO	Cisco
BAC	Bank of America
PFE	Pfizer
LNG	Cheniere Energy

Make notes on your thoughts for each charts.

Try and spend some time on this website and familiarise yourself with the various options for customising your charts.

When you have finished creating the daily charts, try and create and analyse the weekly charts.

Chapter 17

Analysing your Charts

The plans of the diligent lead to plenty, but those of everyone who is hasty, surely to poverty.

- The Bible – Proverbs 21 verse 5

In this chapter we would analyse a few charts and identify what would have been good entries or exits.

Roll Royce plc

- In the above chart Rolls Royce is in a downtrend but looking at the MACD we can see that there are a few buy and sell signals.

- In February, a buy signal was given when the MACD crossed above midline, accompanied with a moving average crossover on the MACD and the RSI rising above 40.

- A sell signal was given in May when the MACD crossed below midline, accompanied by a moving average crossover from the top and a declining RSI.

Try and identify other signals on the chart and write down the reason you think they are valid signals.

===

Barclays plc

- In the chart above, Barclays was in a sideways trend between January and May2008.

- Between May and July it entered into a downtrend. It then rallied a bit but the rally was short lived.

- In May Barclay's share price closed below support. When support is broken, this is a sign that there is a very high probability that the price will continue to fall.

- The breaking of the support level was also accompanied by a moving average crossover on the chart.

Try and identify other signals on the chart and write down the reason you think they are valid signals.

===

Dell Inc

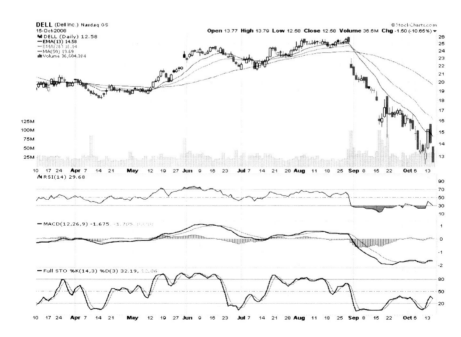

- In the above chart, Dell was in a sideways trend between March and mid May 2008, this was followed by a short-term uptrend which ended in August. A downtrend started at the end of August.

- Around the 12th of May, four indicators produced a buy signal.
  - Stochastics crossed above 50 with both %K and %D rising.
  - There was a moving average crossover on the MACD.
  - RSI is above 50, indicating that average buying is more than selling.
  - On the price chart all the moving averages crossed over to the upside.

- A sell signal was also given in September when there was a gap down. A gap down is usually accompanied with a further fall in price.

Try and identify other signals on the chart and write down the reason you think they are valid signals.

==

Advanced Micro Devices

- In the above chart, a major sell signal was given around the 17th of June.

- On the day before, the price failed to take out a previous high.

- The moving average crossover on the price then gives an indication that the trend is likely to change.

- Further signals are given when the RSI falls below 50, the MACD falls below midline and the Stochastics indicator drops.

Try and identify other signals on the chart and write down the reason you think they are valid signals.

===

Chico FAS, Inc

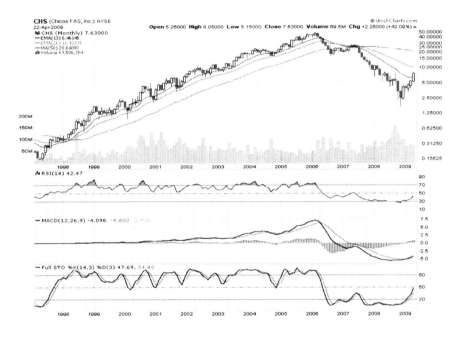

- The above chart is a monthly chart of Chicos FAS, Inc

- A bullish engulfing pattern was formed in November 2008. The bullish engulfing pattern signals the possibility of a change in trend, i.e. from a downtrend to an uptrend.

- In February 2009, the MACD crossed above midline. This cross above midline was accompanied with 12 ma crossing above the 26 ma on the MACD indicator. This is a strong buy signal.

- Further supporting signals are the RSI rising up from below 30, and the Stochastics indicator giving a bullish signal.

Try and identify other signals on the chart and write down the reason you think they are valid signals.

===

Kirkland's, Inc

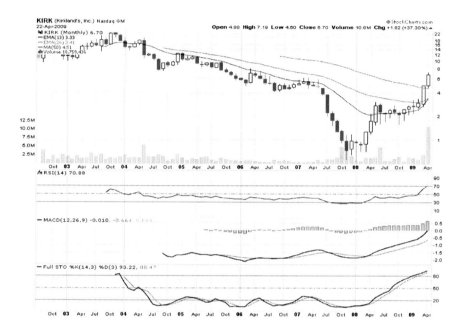

- The above chart is a monthly chart of Kirklands, Inc.

- A bullish engulfing pattern was formed in March 2008. The bullish engulfing pattern signals the possibility of a change in trend, i.e. from a downtrend to an uptrend.

- In April 2008, the MACD crossed above midline. This cross above midline was accompanied with 12 ma crossing above the 26 ma on the MACD indicator. This is a strong buy signal.

- Further supporting signals are the RSI rising up from below 30, and the Stochastics indicator giving a bullish signal.

Try and identify other signals on the chart and write down the reason you think they are valid signals.

===

Wendy's Group, Inc

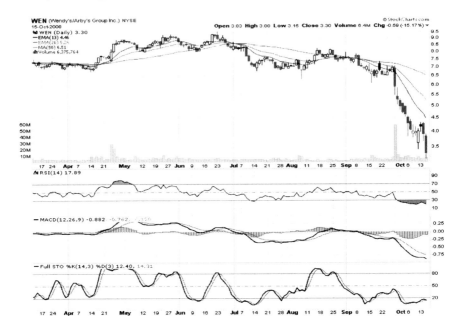

Study the chart above and identify the signals on the chart and write down the reason you think they are valid signals.

Write your answers in the space provided below.

AES Corp

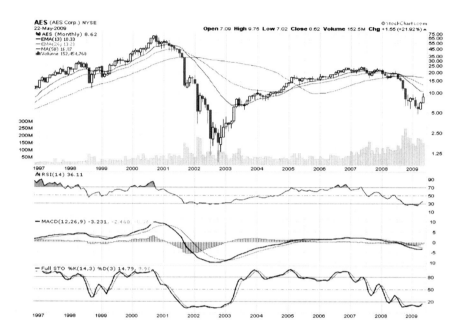

Study the chart above and identify the signals on the chart and write down the reason you think they are valid signals. If you are to buy this stock based on the chart as at the date it was captured (22nd May 2009), would you buy immediately or would you wait for the MACD to cross above midline?

Write your answers in the space provided below.

_____

_____

_____

Chapter 18

The Anatomy of a Trade

"My plan of trading was sound enough and won oftener that it lost. If I had stuck to it I'd have been right perhaps as often as seven out of ten times."

– Jesse Livermore

This chapter uses a couple of examples to illustrate the process of identifying, planning and placing a trade.

Example 1 – Patterson-UTI Energy Inc – Daily Charts

Figure 18.1 is a chart of Patterson-UTI Energy Inc.

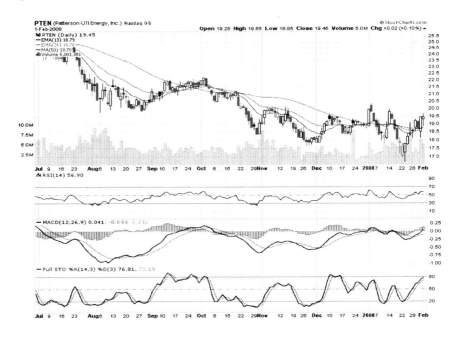

Figure 18.1

The MACD histogram has crossed midline and the current slope of the MACD indicates a bullish trend. RSI is also above midline at

56.90. The 13 and 26 EMA, and the 50 day MA are touching, the 13 EMA is about to cross both the 26 EMA and 50 MA. This shows that there is a high probability of a breakout to the upside. The plan is to buy if the stock takes out the previous high. Since we won't be watching the computer screen all day long, we'll place a buy stop order to buy at $19.70, slightly above the previous high.

Figure 18.2

PTEN opened high, entered the position at $20.20.

Example 2 - Johnson Controls, Inc – Weekly charts

Figure 18.3

The above chart is a weekly chart of Johnson Controls, Inc as at Friday 20th of March 2009. A hammer had formed previous week and the share price of Johnson Controls had continued to rise during the week that ended 20th March. The hammer had signalled a reverse in the trend and the subsequent rise was a confirmation that the trend had potentially reversed. Although RSI had turned upward, the other indicators are yet to give a signal. The best way to enter this position will be to set an order to buy the stock during the week commencing 23rd March if it trades above the high of the previous week, i.e. $11.79. The order should be placed above $11.79, so we'll set it at $11.85.

Figure 18.4

On Monday the 23rd of March, Johnson Controls opens at $11.54 and heads higher above $11.85, to close at $12.62. To cut a long story short, our order is filled and we now own shares in Johnson Controls. That week the stock closes at $12.54.

Since this setup was from the weekly charts, we'll continue to hold the position until we get a sell signal on the weekly charts or until it drops to our stop loss level.

Chapter 19

Spread Betting

Profits can be made safely only when the opportunity is available and not just because they happen to be desired or needed. ...Willingness and ability to hold funds uninvested while awaiting real opportunities is a key to success in the battle for investment survival.- Gerald Loeb

The purpose of this chapter is to introduce spread betting and make you aware of it and the fact that you can use it as a trading tool. It is not intended to cover spreadbetting in detail.

Spreadbetting is a leveraging tool and it is suitable for short to medium term trading. With spreadbetting you do not own the underlying shares that you "buy", you are speculating on the direction of the share price. A lot of people consider spread betting to be gambling, but this is an inaccurate view because the prices that are used in spread betting are the current prices underlying stock in the market. For instance, if I want to buy 500 shares of BP, the price that the share dealing broker would quote for me is the same price that the spread betting broker will quote if I decide to use spread betting to achieve my goal. The advantage of using spread betting is that I would not have to come up with the entire value of the transaction to be able to place the trade. I would only need to pay a margin or fraction of the transaction. This will be illustrated later in this chapter.

With spread betting you can go long and short, which means you can take advantage of price movements in both bull and bear markets. It is a very nice to have tool for traders and investors.

Two other big advantages of spread betting are that under the current UK laws profits made from spread betting are tax-free, and you do not pay commissions and stamp duty to open or close a position.

In addition, with spread betting, some brokers would allow you to use guaranteed stop losses, i.e. you are guaranteed that should the market go against you, your trade will be closed out at the level you specified as your stop loss. A guaranteed stop loss order simply means that you pay a premium for your stop loss price to be guaranteed if there is a gap or slippage in the market.

However, there is a word of warning, spread bets are high-risk products. You need deposit only a small percentage of the value of the position however your losses may substantially exceed that deposit very rapidly and thus require you to make additional deposits at short notice to maintain your bets. Using guaranteed stop losses removes the risk of losing more than you invested.

With spread betting a £1 per penny movement or £1 bet is equivalent to buying 100 shares. This means that for every 1 pence movement you gain £1 or loss £1.

For example let's say I think that the share price of British Airways is going to rise over the next 2 weeks and I want to buy 500 shares of BA to take advantage of the short term movement. I can either buy the shares the traditional way which implies having the full amount for the transaction in my account (i.e. 500 times the share price), or I can use spreadbetting as my investment vehicle by "buying" £5 per point (which is equivalent to 500 shares). Let's say BA is currently trading at 230/232, using spread betting I will deposit £116 (10% of what the total transaction would have cost) to open the trade. If BA is trading at 255/256 four days later and I decide to sell (close) my position, my profit will be (255 – 232)*5 =£115. However, if my prediction is wrong I would lose money.

An analysis of two scenarios is given below;

Scenario 1 (assuming my prediction is correct)

Company: British Airways

Stock Ticker: BAY

Opening position

Date: 23/09/08

Price: 230/232 (i.e. 232 to buy, 230 to sell)

Action: Buy £5 per point. (This is equivalent to buying 500 shares)

Closing Position

Date: 26/09/08

Price: 255/256 (i.e. 256 to buy, 255 to sell)

Action: Sell £5 per point to close the position.

Profit/Loss   23 (255 – 232) * 5 = £115

Scenario 2 (assuming my prediction is wrong)

Company: British Airways

Stock Ticker: BAY

Opening Position

Date: 23/09/08

Quote: 230/232 (i.e. 232 to buy, 230 to sell)

Action: Buy £5 per point. (This is equivalent to buying 500 shares)

Closing Position

Date: 26/09/08

Quote: 210/211 (i.e. 211 to buy, 210 to sell)

Action: Sell £5 per point to close the position.

Profit/Loss   -22 (210 - 232) * 5 = -£110 (A loss)

Rolling and Quarterly Bets

Spreadbetting companies usually quote 2 types of prices (bets) a rolling price and a future price. I wouldn't go into the technical details of what a future price is, but what is important to note is that in spreadbetting you pay a daily interest rate on rolling positions that are carried over to the next day. The rate of interest paid is determined by the spreadbetting company and is applied to your account every night that you hold a position into the next day. However, if you buy a future contract the interest is already added into the spread (quote) and you won't be charged a daily interest. Future contracts are quoted by quarters. There are March, June, September and December future contracts.   The diagram below shows an example of a quote by a spreadbetting company.

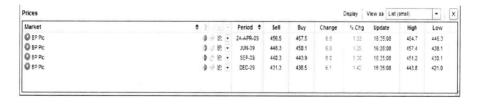

| Prices | | | | Display | View as | List (small) | | ▼ | X |
Market		Period	Sell	Buy	Change	% Chg	Update	High	Low
BP Plc		24-APR-09	456.5	457.5	6.0	1.33	16:35:08	464.7	446.0
BP Plc		JUN-09	448.3	450.1	6.0	1.35	16:35:08	457.4	438.1
BP Plc		SEP-09	440.3	443.9	6.0	1.38	16:35:08	451.2	430.1
BP Plc		DEC-09	431.3	436.5	6.1	1.42	16:35:08	443.8	421.0

If you are going to hold a position for more than 2 weeks it might end up being better to go for a future contract. In fact, if you are using weekly or monthly charts to enter a position you are better off using a future contract. Personally, as most of my positions are intended to be short term to medium trades I use future contracts (prices) with a guaranteed stop loss. Not all spreadbetting providers offer this facility so when opening an account ensure that the provider you intend to do business with offers it.

An illustration of how you can start spread betting with £500

Assuming you have £500 to start investing, if you use the traditional method you might only be able to buy one or two sets of shares. You also have to consider the commissions that you would pay when you buy and when you sell your shares. However, you can take advantage of the leverage that spreadbet offers and you would have the ability to open more than one position. The illustration below shows how you can use £500 to start a spreadbet portfolio.

With spreadbetting it is very important that you need to manage your risk properly. A responsible spreadbetting provider would always remind you that you can lose more than your original deposit. Let's assume that you have £500 to start with, you would not want to lose all your money on one or two trades. You have to decide how much you can afford to risk, or lose if the trade does not go your way. In this illustration we would assume that you do not risk more than 5% of the balance on your account. In the unlikely event that you have 10 consecutive losing trades your account balance would look like the table below;

Balance	Maximum risk allowed	New Balance
500	25	475
475.00	23.75	451.25
451.25	22.56	428.69
428.69	21.43	407.25
407.25	20.36	386.89
386.89	19.34	367.55
367.55	18.38	349.17
349.17	17.46	331.71
331.71	16.59	315.12
315.12	15.76	299.37

This is considered an "unlikely event" because if you have followed the methods and principles within this book, you should not have 10 consecutive losing trades. However, considering the worst case scenario, if this happens you would still have almost £300 in your account.

The maximum risk allowed is the maximum that you should allow yourself to lose if the trade does not go your way. Since this is a percentage of your balance, this amount will increase or decrease as your balance increases or decreases. Assuming your balance is still £500, the maximum you can lose on a trade would be £25. This might mean that you would not be able to buy stocks that have a high price. For instance if you are buying a UK listed share, at this stage you might not be able to buy a stock that cost more than £5 (500p). This is because if you buy a share that costs say £10 (1000p) and you want to risk £25, this means you would have to exit the position if it falls by 25p or 25 points. This is very likely to happen and would be a very bad risk-reward ratio.

If you have a bigger balance, for example £5,000, I'll suggest that you reduce the percentage to 2% or 3%.

Chapter 20

Getting Started

The only way you get a real education in the market is to invest cash, track your trade, and study your mistakes!

Jesse Livermore

Now it's time to put what we have learnt into practice.

First of all you need to know the business hours within which the stock market operates. The UK stock market is open between 8am and 4.30pm GMT time, while the US market is open between 9.30am and 4pm US Eastern time (2.30pm and 9pm GMT time).

Your main goal is to be able to identify quality shares that you can buy (or weak shares that you can short), hold them for a period of time and then sell (or cover) your position and make a profit in the process. The first hurdle is how to identify shares. How do you identify shares that you can review? You can look at the business or financial pages of reputable newspapers and have a look at the companies that are currently in the news. Some of the financial pages also contain a list of shares that had the largest percentage change from the previous day. You can take a note of these shares and use your charts to analyse their performance. You can also buy a magazine that specialises in shares or investments and check out the companies that are being profiled in the issue that you bought. Don't buy a stock just because it was recommended in a magazine, you have to do your own research. If you find any share that you think might be a potential candidate based on the charts, add that share to your watch list. A watch list is list of shares that you are considering buying or shares that you currently own and are monitoring. A watch list can be an Excel spreadsheet or a simple word document. It might even be a manual notepad that you keep. The important thing is that you need to have a watch list. Once you find companies you believe to have potential to meet your selection criteria, place it on your watch list and take note of the behaviour of the stock over time. Also make notes of what you are expecting and the criteria that must be met for you to buy the stock, e.g. a MACD centerline crossover, RSI above 50, or the stock to trade above a previous high etc. The goal is to identify when to take action, and also to ensure you don't take any action if your entry criteria are not met. Once you have your watch list, the frequency that you review it depends on the period of your charts. For daily charts you'll want to review it at least every other day, for weekly charts review weekly (preferable at weekends) and for monthly charts review monthly, at month end.

Resources that you would need

Just as every business requires resources, you would need some basic resources for your investing. You would need;

(1) A personal computer or laptop with an Internet connection, preferably a broadband connection.

(2) Stock market charts, either free ones or one you subscribe to. Although a beginner can get away with using free charting packages, a very active investor might find it easier and convenient using charting packages that cost money to subscribe to. This is because they usually offer more functionality than free packages. When researching what charting package to use remember that the techniques covered in this book do not require that you have intraday prices. Packages that offer intraday prices are usually more expensive. If you are going to use the techniques in this book you only need end-of-day prices. It's also important to note that most brokers offer high quality charting software to their clients.

(3) Microsoft Excel (or similar spreadsheet software) to keep records of your trades and performance.

Selecting a market to trade

You would need to decide on the market or markets that you want to cover. The Internet has made it possible for investors to invest in any stock market in the world without necessarily having to live in that country. For Instance you can live in the United Kingdom and invest in the American stock market; you can also be living in Canada and be able to invest in the UK stock market. Some local brokers allow you to buy international shares but even if you can't get a local broker that will give you access to international share, you can open a trading account online. Just make sure that the company you are opening the account with is a well established company and that it is regulated by country's leading regulatory body, e.g. the financial services authority for UK based companies. It is best to avoid companies that are registered offshore.

Virtual Trading – Real Prices, Pretend Money

If you are a beginner, I'll encourage you to start off with virtual trading. A virtual account is a simulation account and in most cases it simulates real trading. The prices offered are the same as real life prices, although in some instances might be about 15 – 20 minutes delay. The main difference between virtual trading and trading with real money is that your psychology changes when real money is involved. However, if you do not make a profit on your virtual trading, it is highly unlikely that you would make a profit if trading with real money.

Some people (most of them even call themselves experts) claim that virtual trading is useless and you wouldn't achieve anything from using it. Ignore such people. Virtual trading platforms allow you to practise your methods. Like I said earlier, if you don't make a profit on a virtual platform it's very unlikely that you would make a profit on the real platform. I have hardly seen a person that has made a loss in virtual trading and then gone on to make a profit when trading with real money. The reverse is usually true, i.e. people make a profit in virtual trading but then go on to lose money when trading with real money. If you make a profit on the virtual platform, it signifies that your methods are working and you can now work on your psychology. To work on your psychology you have to invest real money. This is because your emotions begin to kick in when you have real money at stake. It's when you have real money at stake that fear and greed kick in. The fear that you might lose all your paper profits if you leave the position a little bit longer, or the greed that you want to double your account balance by the end of the week.

To make virtual trading work for you, treat every virtual trade as a real trade. Have a trading plan for it. For every trade, have a clearly defined buy or sell price and a clearly defined stop loss. When you close a virtual position, write down the reasons for your action.

Practising on a virtual platform is like testing a product in a test environment. The product is only rolled out into real life if it passes the test. Don't start trading your strategy with real money until you are making consistent profits on your virtual trades.

Follow the steps below to start virtual trading;

- Open at least one virtual trading account
  - For UK shares open a virtual trading account on www.bullbearings.co.uk
  - For US Shares open an account on www.virtualstockexchange.com
- Start trading on your virtual accounts.
- Open and close at least 10 positions (over a period).
- Keep documentation of your positions, recording reasons for entering the position and reasons for exit. Also save a copy of the chart on entry and exit.
- Study your trades for lessons learned.
- Ensure that you are regularly making a profit on your virtual accounts before you place a real trade.
- When you start placing real trades, start small.

Opening an Account

When you are ready to start trading with real money you would have to open a trading account. You can search the Internet for online brokers, but make sure that the broker you select is regulated and is an established company. The following are examples of reputable online UK brokers;

E*trade	www.etrade.co.uk
Selftrade	www.selftrade.co.uk
TD Waterhouse	www.tdwaterhouse.co.uk

Examples of reputable online US brokers are;

Optionsxpress	www.optionsxpress.com
E*trade	www.etrade.com
TD Ameritrade	www.tdameritrade.com

Examples of reputable spreadbetting companies are;

IG Index	www.igindex.co.uk
CMC Markets	www.cmcmarkets.co.uk
City Index	www.cityindex.co.uk

Please note that these are just a few examples and I'm not endorsing any of these companies. You have to do your research and find out which ones can offer you the best commission rates, spreads and value for money. Most of them would offer you information on how to use their platforms.

Chapter 21

Food for thought: Extracts from the Diligent Trader blog

This chapter contains a few extracts from my blog. They are included in the book to serve as 'food for thought'.

What is good for the goose is not necessarily good for the gander

I read somewhere that Ed Lampart is adding to his stake in auto parts retailer Autozone and buying shares heavily. For those who don't know him, he is a billionaire hedge fund manager. A couple of weeks ago, Warren Buffett said in a leading US paper that it was time to buy. Does the fact that these 2 people are buying mean that it's time for everyone to buy? In my point of view the answer is no. Don't misunderstand what I'm trying to say. I'm not saying that these guys are wrong in their thinking. I'm not even qualified to say so as I have not made a fraction of the money they have made on the stock market. However, they have a peculiar style of investment and if you are going to follow their advice then you need to make sure that your style is similar to theirs.

Since Buffett made his announcement, the Dow index has fallen over 1000 points, some shares have fallen more than 20%. This is a big drop for a trader or investor that is only willing to hold onto a share provided it doesn't drop more than 10 – 20 % from his entry point. This type of trade won't be suitable for a short term investor.

You also have to think about risk management. Depending on the school of thought (or should I say risk) that you belong to, it's been suggested that to survive as an trader (or even investor) you should not risk more than 5% of your capital on one single stock. Ed Lampart and Warren Buffett have billions at their disposal and can afford to buy shares now and hold onto them till the whole turbulence is over. They are concerned about a company's fundamentals and won't be moved by a 20 or 30% drop in the value of a share price. They know that share prices are heavily discounted at the moment and they are willing to hold onto the shares for as long as it takes. Just consider the following 2 quotes by Warren Buffett

"Our favourite holding period is forever."

"I never attempt to make money on the stock market. I buy on the assumption that they could close the market the next day and not reopen it for five years."

To round up, if you are not happy to hold onto the shares for a long time, don't buy yet. If you are a technical analyst, wait for your charts to give you the signal. That might be tomorrow, next week or next month. Nobody knows when.

Posted 27th October 2008

How are the mighty fallen

No disrespect to the fallen investment banks, but I can't help saying to myself, "how are the mighty fallen". What happened to the big guys? How could the geniuses get it wrong? These are companies that wouldn't employ graduates with less than a second class upper. You had to go to certain schools, or business schools to qualify working for them. A few months ago Bear Sterns had to be bailed out. Over the weekend Merrill Lynch was acquired by Bank of America, while Lehman Brothers filed for Bankruptcy. The unimaginable happened to these guys. These companies were casualties of the subprime mess and the subsequent credit crunch, however their greatest undoing was their irresponsible risk taking. I call it irresponsible because it was excessive and was fed by greed. Nemesis caught up. Goldman Sachs, one of the big investments banks that are still standing had a more conservative policy on risk. They might not have looked like the "shining stars" when other investments banks were taking on the big risk and declaring big profits and bonuses, but the fact that they are still standing, and that there are no doubts about their future is evidence that their responsible risk management is paying off.

The same applies to retail investors. Pigs get slaughtered. It is the one that manages risk properly that stays around for a long time. This might be a time that we all have to review our risk management practises so we can ensure we stay around for a long time. It's not the person that makes a £1000 pounds overnight that is the winner, but the person that makes smaller and steadier profits, accompanied with good risk management.

Posted 15th September 2008

<u>Don't be a master of none</u>

If you have a harem of 40 women, you never get to know any of them very well. – Warren Buffet

To be a successful stock trader/investor you have to limit the number of shares or instruments that you trade. You cannot seize opportunities if you are trying to trade everything that is available across all markets. This might be difficult to grasp if you are a private trader, especially when you want to take advantage of every move across the markets. In investment banks and asset management companies, traders and analyst specialise in particular sectors. This is because the professionals recognise the fact that you cannot be an expert in all sectors. It takes too much energy to focus on too much and the rewards are either little or non-existent. There's a proverb that says "**a jack of all trades, master of none**". You become a master of none when you fail to limit the shares or instruments you want to trade.

Limiting the number of instruments that you trade is very important for beginners. In most cases a beginner wants to be up and running, placing trades and making profit. However, to make and keep your profits you have to be selective in what you trade or invest in. Decide on what you want to focus on, study past patterns, try and identify patterns that repeat themselves, identify the trend, identify the next move etc.

If you've struggled to make a profit in the last month or struggle to hold onto your profits, why don't you give this a try? Create a watchlist of about 20 – 30 instruments. If you want to trade shares on the UK and US markets, select about 10 – 15 shares (including the major indices) from each market, add them into a spreadsheet and study the charts of each of them, making comments where appropriate. This exercise might take a while the first time you do it' but subsequently should not take more than a hour per day. The best time to do this exercise is when the markets are closed.

I'll cover more about how to place your orders in a later post.

Posted 14th August 2008

Do not despise the days of small beginnings

The Bible, Zechariah 4 v 8 -10 "Moreover the word of the LORD came unto me, saying, The hands of Zerubbabel have laid the foundation of this house; his hands shall also finish it; and thou shalt know that the LORD of hosts hath sent me unto you. For who hath despised the day of small things? for they shall rejoice, and shall see the plummet in the hand of Zerubbabel with those seven; they are the eyes of the LORD, which run to and fro through the whole earth.

Do not despise the days of small beginnings is a phrase that we use to encourage one another regularly. However when it comes to the nitty gritty of practising this philosophy, it seems no one wants to live it. We all want to go from zero to hero overnight. Everyone wants to go from amateur to expert within the twinkle of an eye. The media entice us with slogans like from zero to hero, "how to make 1 million in one month" etc. Unfortunately life rarely works this way. There is a process to everything in life. You have to start from somewhere and work your way to the top. Most of the great leaders we know today started from somewhere. Barack Obama didn't end up being a presidential aspirant overnight, he started from the grassroots and worked his way diligently to where he is today. Richard Branson

160

started his business on a small scale and today is one of the greatest entrepreneurs of this generation. Bishop T. D Jakes, the founder of one of the biggest churches in the US didn't arrive at the big scene overnight. If you listen to, or read his story you'll see that he started his preaching with a small congregation and through diligence and faithfulness he was promoted to higher grounds.

Even Warren Buffet, one of the greatest investors of our generation did not become a great investor overnight. He would have started investing with small amounts, gradually increasing it till he got to where he is today. Most people don't even know that he worked for Benjamin Graham, the author of The Intelligent Investor. Through hard work and diligence Warren Buffet has been able to establish himself.

Why am I being a bit philosophical here? The financial markets offer a world of opportunity to people to build wealth, however only a few people are able to seize this opportunity. Many have tried and have had their hands burned, while many are just too scared to try because of stories that they have heard. Why have people had their hands burned and, why are people too scared or just not bothered to try? The main reason is because they do not understand the true meaning of "do not despise the days of small beginnings", i.e. they are just not willing to start small. The get rich overnight mentality doesn't help matters. A lot of training courses take advantage of human greed by selling you slogans like "how to turn £3,000 into £36,000 in 6 weeks", or "how to make a million in the stock market". People see these adverts and then rush to register for such courses, paying thousands of pounds, with the hope of recouping their training fees within a few weeks. The end result is usually disappointment. Can an absolute beginner turn £3,000 into £36,000 in 6 weeks? I won't say impossible, but certainly, it's unlikely. To do that, it's 99% certain that person violated all rules of money management.

Are you new to investing via the financial markets? Is it something that you have heard about but are too scared to start? I'll challenge/encourage you to start small and see how you'll progress onto being great. Start off by buying 100 shares instead of 1000 or speculating £1 per point instead of £10. If you can't make money consistently risking £20, how on earth can you honestly expect to make money risking £200 a trade? Diligenttrader encourages people to start small.

Posted 4th July 2008

How much more downside is there in this market?

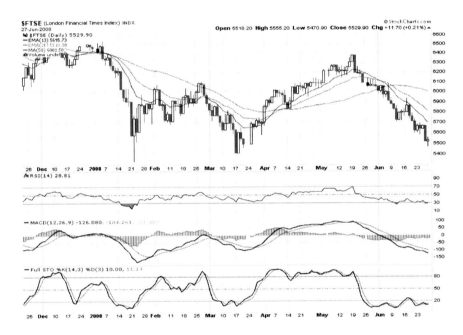

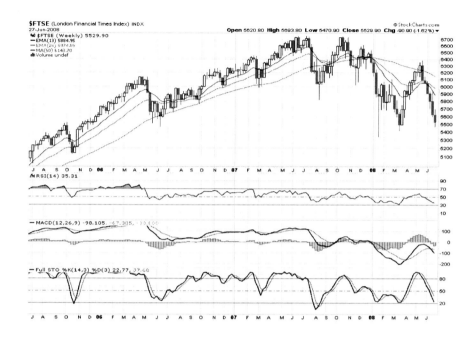

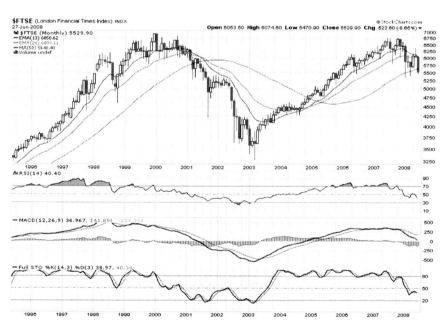

Share prices have been falling for a while. The short-term and intermediate term trends are to the downside. How much lower can share prices go? Have they fallen far enough? To answer this question one has to look at the longer term charts, i.e. weekly and monthly.

While looking at the daily chart of the FTSE 100, it appears to be oversold. RSI is below 30 and stochastic is below 20. Although we have oversold signals on the chart, there are no reversal signals on it. Hence, now is not the time to buy, especially if you are buying for the short-term.

On the weekly chart we see that the FTSE 100 is approaching/sitting on support at 5500. However if we look at the indicators, RSI is around 35 and still heading down. This signifies selling is winning the battle. A look at the MACD indicator shows that the faster moving average has just crossed the slower one moving down and that the histogram has crossed below zero. This means there is more downside.

On the monthly chart, we see a bearish candle and the Index has closed below the 50 day moving average for the first time since 2004. The left side of chart show that something similar happened in 2001. All three indicators on the monthly chart are showing sell signals.

Even though the daily chart is showing signs of the market being oversold, the weekly and monthly charts are showing that there is still some downside.

Let's remember the indicators and charts are there to show us a picture of what is currently happening in the market, they do not provide a 100% assurance of what would happen. The unforeseen such as government intervention, central bank cash injections etc, can still happen and can cause the market to act contrary to the signals generated by the charts. Let's also note that even if a market is in a downtrend, you can still have the occasional days or weeks where the market will go up before resuming its downtrend. Lastly, even when the overall market is in a downtrend, there would still be some sectors or companies that will experience an uptrend within the overall downtrend. There will also be opportunities for short-selling.

My analysis is that until there is evidence to the contrary, there is still some downside in this market, even though you need to be cautious as the index might make one more attempt to rally above the 50 day MA on the monthly chart. However there is money to be made, irrespective of whether the market is going up or down.

Posted 30th June 2008

Conclusion

"When you want to test the depths of a stream, don't use both feet."

Chinese proverb

You've probably seen a lot of advertisements telling you that you can double your money in a month through trading. Unfortunately we live in a "microwave" generation and most people fall for these claims. People are not ready to go through the process to become a great trader/investor.

Investing in the stock market is like a sport. A lot of preparation and training takes place in the background before the athlete begins to experience great results. For example, Tiger Woods is one of the greatest golfers around at the moment. Most people want to become Tiger Woods overnight, forgetting that Tiger Woods started playing golf as a child, and that he had to put in a lot of hours developing his skill. He also had to train his mind and discipline himself. New sports stars arrive on the scene regularly. In 2007, Lewis Hamilton was the sports sensation of the year and sometime this year (2009) we will be introduced to a new sports sensation. Whatever the sport the person happens to be involved in, we need to realise that the person would not have become a sensation overnight. It's most likely that the person would have spent a lot of time preparing for that "moment in time". The person would have made a lot of sacrifices in terms of the time spent training and also in terms of disciplining themselves.

Whatever career or occupation that you are in now, you would not have achieved overnight success. Even if you have outperformed compared to your colleagues, you would have had to start from somewhere. A doctor would not be expected, or even allowed to perform life threatening surgery on a patient shortly after qualifying. An accountant would not be expected to oversee a multi-million account too soon after qualifying. There's a big difference between text book knowledge and experience. Although in most professions you need the "text book knowledge" background before you can develop the experience.

Let's bring our discussion back to trading and investing. Do you think that a rookie trader in an investment bank will be expected to double his account in his first year? The answer is no. Even though investment banks and hedge funds are seen as aggressive and expect results from their traders, they understand that the new trader has to spend time getting familiar with his tools and developing himself in other areas.

People need to develop their technical skills and also their trading psychology. These two aspects of trading take time to master. You need to build your confidence and your belief in yourself. You need to identify your weakness and work on it. You need to identify what works for you and what doesn't. You need to start off with small position sizes. This allows you to work on your psychology because you have not overexposed yourself and the small losses that might appear on your statement will not impair your judgment. For example, let's say you buy 200 shares of Barclays at 500p per share. Your total spend will be £1,000. Let's say the share price fall to 490p, your investment will have fallen to £980, indicating a paper loss of £20. If you bought 1,000 share, if Barclays falls to 490p, your paper loss will be £100. At this point, considering the fact that you are a beginner and you haven't got much experience to draw from, looking at a £100 paper loss can cause you to panic and make you close out your position before it reaches its stop loss. However, as you gain experience you'll discover that shares have a way of pulling back before they shoot up and you will be able to hold yourself back from selling before the price violates your stop-loss. When you start trading you should be concerned about getting it right, rather than making a killing on the trade. Concentrate on getting it right and profit will look after itself.

Don't underestimate the power of your journal

We've talked about the importance of a trading journal, but I think it is important to mention it once again. It's important that you have a record for every trade you place, or every investment that you make. Your journal should state the reasons why you placed the trade, what you are trying to achieve, where you think the share price is heading etc.

The front page of your journal should state the criteria that should be met before you buy, sell or short a stock. Your individual entries into the journal should specify whether your criteria were met or whether you violated your criteria. It should also contain your plan for each trade, and after you have placed the trade you should make a record of whether you placed the trade according your plan, or not.

You should also perform a regular review of your performance. The frequency of the review can be weekly, monthly, quarterly, etc., depending on how active you are. You should review your win/loss ratio, i.e. number of winning positions to number of losing positions and try and identify the cause of the losing positions. You also need to review the number of planned trades versus number of unplanned trades.

It would be virtually impossible to perform these reviews and analysis without a journal or a record of your activity. Start keeping a journal now so that it becomes a habit. If you don't get into the habit of keeping a journal, you get into the habit of not keeping a journal. As you would know, habits can be difficult to break.

The man who wanted to win the lottery

I once heard a story about a man who wanted to become a millionaire by winning the lottery. Every Saturday night just before the draw, the man would pray to God for favour to win and after the draw he was always disappointed. This went on for about a year. Then one Saturday night as the man prayed that his numbers would come up that night, he heard a voice. God said to him, "David why don't you meet me half way, at least buy a lottery ticket and then you can pray that your numbers are drawn as the winning numbers". The morale of the story is that if you want to win the lottery, the least you can do is to buy your lottery ticket. Nothing happens until you act. If you want to make money on the stock market you have to take action.

Can you succeed in the stock market?

"With persistence and hard work anything is possible. You can do it, and your own determination to succeed is the most important element" – William J. O'Neil.

Most people know Tiger Woods as one of the greatest golfers of all times. One of his first major wins was the Masters in Augusta in 1997. What most people don't realise is that he didn't win by just playing a few rounds at Augusta. Prior to taking part in the game, he studied the previous year's videotapes. He watched and analysed how the greens were laid out and how to hit the ball from every position. Tiger Woods put in many hours of practice. His practice paid off by winning trophies. How does this apply to you? In the beginning you have to study and analyse numerous charts, you have to understand how share prices react to different indicators and scenarios.

Do not despise the days of small beginnings

"The man who removes a mountain begins by carrying away small stones."

Chinese proverb

In conclusion, I'm urging you not to despise the days of small beginnings. Start small and concentrate on getting it right rather than the millions you can potentially make from trading. As you begin to get positive results you can increase your position sizes, thereby also increasing your profits. You are welcome to share your results and experience with me. Just email me at admin@diligenttrader.com.

All the best.

Appendix 1

Useful Web sites

www.diligenttrader.com

www.stockcharts.com

www.moneyam.com

www.bloomberg.co.uk

www.bloomberg.com

www.reuters.co.uk

www.bigcharts.com

www.bullbearings.co.uk

www.virtualstockexchange.com

www.optionsxpress.eu

http://www.igindex.co.uk

http://finance.google.co.uk/finance

http://finance.google.com/finance

Appendix 2

The following table contains the components of the FTSE 100 as at the 26th of June 2009.

Name	Symbol		Name	Symbol
ANGLO AMERICAN	AAL.L		KAZAKHMYS	KAZ.L
ASSOCIAT BRIT FOODS	ABF.L		KINGFISHER	KGF.L
ADMIRAL GROUP	ADM.L		LAND SEC R.E.I.T.	LAND.L
AMEC	AMEC.L		LEGAL & GENERAL	LGEN.L
ANTOFAGASTA	ANTO.L		LIBERTY INT R.E.I.T	LII.L
ALLIANCE TRUST	ATST.L		LLOYDS BANKING GRP	LLOY.L
AUTONOMY CORP	AU.L		LONMIN	LMI.L
AVIVA	AV.L		LSE GROUP	LSE.L
ASTRAZENECA	AZN.L		MARKS & SPENCER	MKS.L
BAE SYSTEMS	BA.L		MORRISON SUPERMKTS	MRW.L
BARCLAYS	BARC.L		NATIONAL GRID	NG.L
BRIT AMER TOBACCO	BATS.L		NEXT	NXT.L
BRITISH AIRWAYS	BAY.L		OLD MUTUAL	OML.L
BG GROUP	BG.L		PETROFAC	PFC.L
BRIT LAND CO REIT	BLND.L		PENNON GRP	PNN.L
BHP BILLITON	BLT.L		PRUDENTIAL	PRU.L
BUNZL	BNZL.L		PEARSON	PSON.L
BP	BP.L		RECKITT BENCK GRP	RB.L
B SKY B GROUP	BSY.L		ROYAL BK SCOTL GR	RBS.L
BT GROUP	BT.L		ROYAL DUTCH SHELL-A	RDSA.L
CADBURY ADR	CBRY.L		REED ELSEVIER	REL.L
CARNIVAL	CCL.L		REXAM	REX.L
CENTRICA	CNA.L		RIO TINTO	RIO.L
CAIRN ENERGY	CNE.L		ROLLS-ROYCE GROUP	RR.L
COBHAM	COB.L		RANDGOLD RESOURCES	RRS.L
COMPASS GROUP	CPG.L		RSA INSUR GRP	RSA.L
CAPITA GRP	CPI.L		SABMILLER	SAB.L

Name	Symbol	Name	Symbol
CABLE & WIRELESS	CW.L	SAINSBURY	SBRY.L
DIAGEO	DGE.L	SCHRODERS	SDR.L
MAN GROUP	EMG.L	SCHRODERS NVTG	SDRC.L
EURASIAN NATURAL	ENRC.L	SAGE GRP	SGE.L
EXPERIAN	EXPN.L	SHIRE	SHP.L
FRIENDS PROV GRP	FP.L	STANDARD LIFE	SL.L
FOREIGN&COL INV TST	FRCL.L	SMITHS GROUP	SMIN.L
FRESNILLO	FRES.L	SMITH & NEPHEW	SN.L
G4S	GFS.L	SERCO GROUP	SRP.L
GLAXOSMITHKLINE	GSK.L	SCOT & STHN ENERGY	SSE.L
HAMMERSON REIT	HMSO.L	STANDARD CHARTERED	STAN.L
HOME RETAIL GROUP	HOME.L	SEVERN TRENT	SVT.L
HSBC HLDG	HSBA.L	THOMAS COOK GRP	TCG.L
ICAP	IAP.L	TULLOW OIL	TLW.L
INTERCONT HOTELS	IHG.L	THOMSON REUTERS	TRIL.L
3I GROUP	III.L	TESCO PLC	TSCO.L
IMPERIAL TOBACCO	IMT.L	TUI TRAVEL	TT.L
INTERNATIONAL POWER	IPR.L	UNILEVER	ULVR.L
INMARSAT	ISAT.L	UNITED UTILITIES GR	UU.L
INVENSYS	ISYS.L	VEDANTA RESOURCES	VED.L
INTERTEK GROUP	ITRK.L	VODAFONE GRP	VOD.L
JOHNSON MATTHEY PLC	JMAT.L	WOLSELEY	WOS.L

Appendix 3

The "build a £1000 portfolio" challenge

Did you know that if you open a spreadbetting account with £1000 and aim to achieve a 10% return every month, you can turn your initial deposit into over £300,000 in 5 years? Just look at the table below and see how £1000 can build up to become over £300,000.

Month	Portfolio value at the start of the month	Portfolio value at the end of the month	Month	Portfolio value at the start of the month	Portfolio value at the end of the month
Month 1	1000	1100	Month 31	17449.4	19194.34
Month 2	1100	1210	Month 32	19194.34	21113.78
Month 3	1210	1331	Month 33	21113.78	23225.15
Month 4	1331	1464.1	Month 34	23225.15	25547.67
Month 5	1464.1	1610.51	Month 35	25547.67	28102.44
Month 6	1610.51	1771.561	Month 36	28102.44	30912.68
Month 7	1771.561	1948.717	Month 37	30912.68	34003.95
Month 8	1948.717	2143.589	Month 38	34003.95	37404.34
Month 9	2143.589	2357.948	Month 39	37404.34	41144.78
Month 10	2357.948	2593.742	Month 40	41144.78	45259.26
Month 11	2593.742	2853.117	Month 41	45259.26	49785.18
Month 12	2853.117	3138.428	Month 42	49785.18	54763.7
Month 13	3138.428	3452.271	Month 43	54763.7	60240.07
Month 14	3452.271	3797.498	Month 44	60240.07	66264.08
Month 15	3797.498	4177.248	Month 45	66264.08	72890.48
Month 16	4177.248	4594.973	Month 46	72890.48	80179.53
Month 17	4594.973	5054.47	Month 47	80179.53	88197.49
Month 18	5054.47	5559.917	Month 48	88197.49	97017.23
Month 19	5559.917	6115.909	Month 49	97017.23	106719
Month 20	6115.909	6727.5	Month 50	106719	117390.9
Month 21	6727.5	7400.25	Month 51	117390.9	129129.9
Month 22	7400.25	8140.275	Month 52	129129.9	142042.9

Month	Portfolio value at the start of the month	Portfolio value at the end of the month	Month	Portfolio value at the start of the month	Portfolio value at the end of the month
Month 23	8140.275	8954.302	Month 53	142042.9	156247.2
Month 24	8954.302	9849.733	Month 54	156247.2	171871.9
Month 25	9849.733	10834.71	Month 55	171871.9	189059.1
Month 26	10834.71	11918.18	Month 56	189059.1	207965.1
Month 27	11918.18	13109.99	Month 57	207965.1	228761.6
Month 28	13109.99	14420.99	Month 58	228761.6	251637.7
Month 29	14420.99	15863.09	Month 59	251637.7	276801.5
Month 30	15863.09	17449.4	Month 60	276801.5	304481.6

I'll like to invite you to take the challenge. If you are interested, send an email to admin@diligenttrader.com, typing £1000 challenge in the heading and you'll get instructions on how to take part in the challenge. Don't worry I won't be taking any money from you and you would have full control of your account.

Index

Lightning Source UK Ltd.
Milton Keynes UK
11 April 2011

170712UK00001B/12/P

9 780956 424709